motorcycle
riding
the essential skills

Approved by
Plain
English
Campaign

London: TSO

Published with the permission of the Driving Standards Agency on behalf of the Controller of Her Majesty's Stationery Office.

© Crown copyright 2001.

First edition Crown copyright 1991
Second edition Crown copyright 1996
Third edition Crown Copyright 1999
Fourth edition Crown Copyright 2001
Fourth impression 2001
Fifth impression 2002

ISBN 0 11 552257 3

A CIP catalogue record for this book is available from the British Library.

Other titles in the Driving Skills series

The Official Theory Test for Motorcyclists

The Official Theory Test for Car Drivers

The Official Theory Test for Drivers of Large Vehicles

Driving: the Essential Skills

The Official Driving Test

The Official Guide to Accompanying L-drivers

Driving Buses and Coaches: the Official DSA Syllabus

Driving Goods Vehicles: the Official DSA Syllabus

The Official Tractor and Specialist Vehicle Driving Tests

The Official Theory Test (CD-ROM)

The Official DSA Guide for Driving Instructors

Official Motorcycling – CBT, Theory & Practical Test

Acknowledgements

The Driving Standards Agency (DSA) would like to thank the staff of the Department for Transport, Local Government and the Regions for their contribution to the production of this publication.

Every effort has been made to ensure that the information contained in this publication is accurate at the time of going to press. The Stationery Office cannot be held responsible for any inaccuracies. Information in this book is for guidance only.

The Driving Standards Agency (DSA) is an executive agency of the Department of the Environment, Transport and the Regions.

You'll see its logo at test centres.

DSA aims to promote road safety through the advancement of driving standards by

- establishing and developing high standards and best practice in driving and riding on the road; before people start to drive, as they learn, and after they pass their test
- ensuring high standards of instruction for different types of driver and rider
- conducting the statutory theory and practical tests efficiently, fairly and consistently across the country
- providing a centre of excellence for driver training and driving standards
- develop a range of publications and other publicity material designed to promote safe driving for life.

DSA Website

www.driving-tests.co.uk

DTLR Website

www.dtlr.gov.uk

Green Issues Website

www.defra.gov.uk/environment/index.htm

CONTENTS

Motorcycling can be a pleasant and exhilarating experience, as well as an economic means of transport. However, the volume of traffic and faster, more powerful motorcycles make it essential, more than ever before, for riders to be ready to deal with the unexpected and question the actions of other road users. After all, it's in your interest to make safety *your* responsibility.

Whether you're an experienced motorcyclist or a new rider you'll realise that riding not only requires skill in handling your machine but also the ability to 'read' the road. Good observation and anticipation are essential to safe riding.

This book is a step-by-step guide to motorcycling, covering all aspects: from choosing your machine and the correct protective clothing to defensive riding and the importance of proper training. It's an essential reference book for all motorcyclists, however experienced – instructors too. Read it carefully and put into practice the advice it gives.

Above all, make sure that your aim is *'Safe riding for life'*.

Robin Cummins

Chief Driving Examiner
Driving Standards Agency

Riding a motorcycle can be great fun and is enjoyed by people of all ages. However, riding on the road means accepting responsibility for yourself and showing due care and consideration for all other road users.

Compared with driving other road vehicles, riding a motorcycle puts you at greater risk from other road users. If you're involved in an accident the chances of being injured are **very** high.

The machine, the special clothing, the road, the weather, and the traffic are all part of the environment of motorcycling. How well you get on depends on *you*.

This part covers the attitude and approach you need to ensure that you enjoy a long and safe motorcycling career.

The topics covered

- your attitude
- new riders
- returning riders
- expertise
- economy.

Your attitude

A good rider isn't a perfect rider; it's very doubtful if such a rider exists. A good rider always tries to set a good example by showing

- responsibility
- anticipation
- patience
- concentration
- expertise.

Together, these qualities go to make up what is generally known as the rider's attitude. The importance of attitude to safe riding cannot be stressed enough. The attitude **you** take to motorcycling will influence the type of rider you become.

Take pride in your riding and you'll develop a positive attitude. This won't always be easy, but keep working at it.

It's a fact that nearly all road accidents are caused by human error. Reducing that risk is the responsibility of us all.

Responsibility

To be a responsible rider you should always be concerned for the safety of all road users.

This includes

- yourself and your passenger
- other drivers and riders
- cyclists
- pedestrians, particularly the most vulnerable such as
  - children
  - the elderly
  - people with disabilities.

Be responsible by recognising your own limitations. Riding beyond the bounds of caution is foolish and irresponsible.

Develop the right attitude from the beginning and you'll become a safe and responsible rider.

Anticipation

When you're riding a motorcycle it's vital that you plan ahead. This means acting before situations get out of control. As a motorcyclist you have to consider

- other road users. They don't always do what you expect. Question their actions and be ready for the unexpected
- the road. How sharp is the next bend? What's around the next corner? Can you stop within your range of vision? Road signs and road markings are there to help you plan ahead
- the conditions. You'll be exposed to the weather and affected by the road conditions. Slippery surfaces are especially dangerous for motorcyclists.

Always ask yourself the question 'What if...?'

DSA MOTORCYCLE RIDING

Patience

Try not to over-react if another road user does something wrong. Control your desire to retaliate. Everyone can make a mistake, including you. You should make allowances for other people's mistakes just as you'd want them to make allowances for yours.

Showing good manners is the hallmark of a skilful rider. Others will learn from watching you and will appreciate your courtesy and good riding.

Traffic jams and delays can cause frustration. Avoid the need to rush. Set out with plenty of time to spare. It's always better to arrive late than not at all.

Concentration

Riding on today's roads demands full concentration.

If you're driving a car a lapse in concentration may only dent your pride (and your car). Motorcycles aren't so forgiving. Your survival will depend on your concentration.

Many factors can disrupt your concentration such as

- fatigue
- feeling unwell
- being cold or wet
- worries
- alcohol
- drugs.

It's in your own interest not to ride if you know you can't concentrate fully.

Fatigue Tiredness can creep up on anyone and may go unnoticed until it is too late. Boredom or monotony can aid the onset of fatigue such as when riding

- at night
- in fog
- on motorways.

The likelihood of suffering from fatigue may be further increased by

- chilling effects of the weather
- noise and vibration.

Wearing ear plugs helps to reduce noise and prevent hearing damage while specialist motorcycle clothing will give the best protection from the elements.

Don't start a journey if you're already feeling tired. If you feel tired while riding stop at a safe place and rest until you feel you can continue safely.

On a motorway rest at the nearest service area or leave the motorway. Do not pull up on the hard shoulder just to rest.

When you plan your journey remember to include time for breaks and refreshment.

Remember...tiredness kills.

Tiredness Can Kill
Take A Break

Feeling unwell Health is one personal matter which can upset your concentration. A bad cold can distract your mind and slow your reactions. If you feel tired or unwell don't ride.

Cold and wet Without proper clothing you can get very cold and wet when riding a motorcycle. Hands and feet are especially susceptible. Being cold and wet will reduce your ability to concentrate and slow your reactions.

Worries If something upsets or worries you think twice before starting a journey. If you can't concentrate on your riding consider using some other means of transport.

Alcohol This will reduce your ability to ride safely. The law sets the limit of 80 milligrams of alcohol per 100 millilitres of blood. It's an offence to ride a motorcycle or a moped if you exceed this level.

If you want to be safe and you're going to ride don't drink at all.

Drugs Taking certain drugs is a criminal offence. Riding when you're under their influence can seriously impair your concentration, and the outcome could be fatal.

If your doctor prescribes medicines for you, ask if they'll affect your ability to ride safely. Some over-the-counter medicines can also affect you. Read the label. If in doubt ask the chemist or your doctor.

The responsibility is yours.

Warning

Riding under the influence of alcohol or drugs could invalidate your insurance.

Warning: May cause drowsiness. If affected, **don't drive.**

New riders

Young and inexperienced motorcyclists are more vulnerable on the roads. They can often be involved in accidents early in their motorcycling careers, sometimes tragically so. Such accidents can usually be attributed to

- the natural exuberance of youth
- immaturity; an inability to cope with the serious nature of riding a motorcycle
- showing off
- competitive behaviour, racing and so on
- lack of experience and judgement
- being over-confident of their own ability.

Avoid

- riding too fast; speed can kill
- riding without consideration and care
- showing off; if you want to impress your friends, show them how **safe** a motorcyclist you are
- being 'wound up'; keep calm, learn to ignore the stupidity of others
- an aggressive attitude and behaviour
- riding beyond your capabilities; always leave yourself a safety margin
- being distracted.

Do

- above all, be responsible and always show courtesy and consideration to other road users. Your life, and the lives of others, could depend on it!
- be safe, don't take risks!

False perceptions

Many young and inexperienced motorcyclists **wrongly** believe that the ability to handle their motorcycle will make them a good and safe rider. They fail to recognise that handling skill alone will not prevent accidents.

Having the right attitude of mind and a sound knowledge of defensive riding techniques is essential.

Returning riders

If you return to motorcycling after an absence of several years you'll probably find a lot has changed. This will include

- road and traffic conditions
- motorcycle technology
- your skills.

While you may continue to hold your full motorcycle licence from years ago it's recommended that you seek refresher training before taking to the road on a motorcycle. Most Approved Training Bodies (ATBs) can provide this training and it's a good way to refresh your skills in a safe and enjoyable manner. You can find a local ATB from

- yellow pages
- local newspapers
- your motorcycle dealer.

Expertise

Master the techniques set out in this manual. They were developed by experienced riders and they make sense.

Develop safe habits and a responsible attitude from the very beginning. Always think about how other road users will be affected by your actions.

Think 'safety'.

Start-up costs

Deposit   £ __
Clothing   £ __
Boots   £ __
Helmet   £ __
Training

Budget

Monthly loan
repayments (x 12)
'Road Tax'   £ __
Insurance   £ __
Petrol   £ __
Oil   £ __
Maintenance   £ __
Tyres   £ __
Misc.   £ __
Total for year   £ __
Monthly cost   £ __
                        £ __

Economy

Motorcycling is traditionally a cheap form of transport, but running some modern motorcycles can be more expensive than running some types of car. However, if you're a beginner you must accept that there are considerable start-up costs.

Don't cut costs to below the minimum level of safety. For example, don't risk using worn or damaged tyres. Safety must never be sacrificed for economy.

Set yourself a budget so that you know what you can afford. This will help you to identify where savings can be made.

You'll have to consider the

- purchase price of the motorcycle
- vehicle excise duty and insurance
- cost of proper clothing and a safety helmet
- cost of training
- running costs: fuel, maintenance, etc.

You have to comply with certain legal requirements before you can ride on the road. These cover:

- you
- your motorcycle.

Most of the requirements are there to protect you and other road users. If you neglect them you could face serious penalties. Complying with the law isn't cheap but failing to comply could turn out to be much more expensive.

The topics covered

- motorcycle riders
- theory test
- moped riders
- compulsory basic training (CBT)
- foreign licence holders
- disqualified riders
- New Drivers Act
- vehicle documents
- insurance.

Motorcycle riders

To ride a motorcycle on the road you must be at least 17 years old and hold a driving licence which allows you to ride motorcycles (Category A).

That licence can be any of the following

- a provisional driving licence. This provides provisional car, motorcycle and moped entitlement
- a full category A motorcycle licence
- a full sub-category A1 light motorcycle licence
- a full car licence. This provides provisional motorcycle entitlement
- a full moped licence. This provides provisional motorcycle entitlement.

All riders must

- wear a safety helmet at all times when riding unless they are a member of the Sikh religion and wear a turban
- ensure any helmet visor used conforms to BSI or EU standards. (See Part four, 'visors and goggles')

Provisional motorcycle entitlement

After completing Compulsory Basic Training (CBT) (see 'Compulsory Basic Training' later in this part) learners may ride a solo motorcycle

- up to 125 cc
- with a power output of no more than 11 kW.

Note

From 1 February 2001 provisional driving licences will be issued with provisional motorcycle entitlement valid for the life of the licence (subject to holding a valid CBT certificate).

Provisional motorcycle licences issued before 1 February 2001 required the practical motorcycle test to be passed within two years of the date of issue or motorcycle entitlement would be withdrawn for one year. From 1 February 2001 these licence holders may

- apply for a replacement licence at the end of two years without a 12-month waiting period. The replacement licence will be issued until age 70.

- apply for a replacement licence immediately if the licence has already expired under the two-year rule. The replacement licence will be issued until age 70.
- apply for a replacement licence immediately if the licence has been surrendered to preserve the balance of the two years. The replacement licence will be issued until age 70.

Driving licence application forms are available from

- Post Offices
- Traffic Area Offices
- Vehicle Registration Offices
- Driver and Vehicle Licensing Agency (DVLA).

Learners who wish to ride a sidecar outfit can do so as long as it has a power to weight ratio not exceeding 0.16 kW/kg.

With provisional motorcycle entitlement you must not

- ride on motorways
- carry a pillion passenger
- ride without red L-plates fitted to both front and rear of the motorcycle. In Wales you may display red D-plates (for *dysgwr*, the Welsh for 'learner'). If you cross from Wales into another part of the United Kingdom you must display L-plates.

Full motorcycle licence

There are two types of full motorcycle licence

- sub-category A1-light motorcycle licence.
- category A-standard motorcycle licence.

Sub-category A1

A full A1 licence allows you to ride machines up to 125 cc and with a power output of up to 11 kW (14.6 bhp).

You can obtain a full sub-category A1 licence by passing the practical test on a bike of between 75 cc and 125 cc.

**Test motorcycle to obtain a
light motorcycle licence**

Category A

A full category A licence gives you full entitlement to all machines.

You can obtain a full category A licence

- with a two year qualifying period
- without a two year qualifying period via Direct Access (see below).

121-125cc capable of at least 100kph

**Test motorcycle to obtain a
standard motorcycle licence**

Category A with 2 year qualifying period
This will be obtained by passing the motorcycle test on a motorcycle of between 121 cc and 125 cc and capable of at least 100 kph (62.5 mph).

Riders who are subject to the two year qualifying period will be restricted to

Theory Test

From 1 February 2001 all candidates for a practical motorcycle test must first pass a motorcycle theory test, unless

- upgrading from A1 to A
- a full moped licence is held which was obtained by pasing the moped test after 1 July 1996.

DSA MOTORCYCLE RIDING

machines of 25 kW (33 bhp) maximum or power to weight ratio not exceeding 0.16 kW/kg for two years from the date of passing their test. At the end of that time any size of motorcycle may be ridden without taking another test.

Category A via Direct Access This is for riders aged 21 or over. Passing the motorcycle test on a machine of at least 35 kW (46.6 bhp) gives immediate access to all sizes of motorcycle.

You can practise on any size of motorcycle which exceeds the UK learner specification provided that

- you are accompanied at all times by a qualified approved instructor, on another motorcycle and in radio contact
- fluorescent or reflective safety clothing is worn during supervision
- L-plates (D-plates in Wales) are fitted and provisional licence restrictions followed.

Test motorcycles

- motorcycles less than 75 cc aren't acceptable for the practical motorcycle test
- only the disabled can use a motorcycle and sidecar combination for the test. The licence obtained will be restricted to such combinations
- if you pass your test on a motorcycle with automatic or semi-automatic transmission this will be recorded on your licence. Your full licence entitlement will be restricted to motorcycles in this category.

Accelerated Access This option is for riders over 21 years old or who reach the age of 21 before their two-year qualifying period is complete.

You can take a further test to give you immediate access to all motorcycles. This test must be taken on a motorcycle with a power output of at least 35 kW (46.6 bhp).

You can practise for this test on motorcycles above 25 kW (33 bhp) provided

- you're accompanied at all times by an approved instructor, on another motorcycle and in radio contact
- fluorescent or reflective safety clothing is worn during supervision
- L-plates (or D-plates in Wales) are fitted and provisional licence restrictions followed.

Full licence entitlement

With a full motorcycle licence you may

- ride without L-plates (or D-plates in Wales)
- carry a pillion passenger
- use motorways.

**Test motorcycle for
Direct and Accelerated access**

Moped riders

To ride a moped on the road you must be at least 16 years old and have a driving licence that entitles you to ride mopeds (Category P).

At 16 but under 17 this can be a

- full moped licence
- provisional moped licence.

At 17 and over it can also be a

- full car licence (see below)
- full motorcycle licence
- provisional driving licence. This provides provisional moped entitlement.

Provisional moped entitlement

After completing CBT this allows you to ride a moped. You must not

- carry a pillion passenger.
- ride without L-plates (or D-plates in Wales) fitted to both the front and the rear of the moped
- ride on motorways.

Full moped licence

Full moped entitlement allows you to

- ride mopeds without L-plates
- carry a pillion passenger.

Remember Mopeds are not allowed to use motorways, even if you hold a full licence.

Full car licence holders

Holders of a full car licence obtained by passing their driving test before 1 February 2001 hold unconditional full moped entitlement.

Holders of a full car licence obtained by passing their driving test on or after 1 February 2001, who do not already hold a full moped or motorcycle licence, must hold a valid CBT completion certificate (DL196) to validate their full moped entitlement.

If a valid DL196 is already held when the car test is passed, the full moped entitlement will be validated immediately.

A DL196 validating full moped entitlement on a full car licence will remain valid for mopeds, for the life of the licence. It is therefore particularly important that the DL196 is kept safe.

Remember the same DL196 that validates your full moped entitlement will have a limited life (see Certificate life) for validating provisional motorcycle entitlement.

Mopeds

- have an engine under 50 cc
- don't weigh more than 250 kg
- if registered before 1 August 1977, can be moved by pedals
- if registered after 1 August 1977, have a maximum design speed not exceeding 50 kph (31 mph).

Compulsory Basic Training (CBT)

CBT is a course of compulsory basic training which all learner motorcycle and moped riders must complete before riding on the road.

CBT can only be given by Approved Training Bodies (ATBs) who have

- instructors that have been assessed by DSA
- sites approved by DSA for off-road training.

CBT allows you to safely learn

- motorcycling theory
- skills which will make you safe on the road
- the correct attitude towards motorcycling.

Many people find CBT is an enjoyable activity and an opportunity to meet like-minded motorcyclists.

You don't have to take CBT if you

- passed a full moped test after 1 December 1990
- live and ride on specified offshore islands
- already hold a valid Certificate of Completion (DL196) obtained during a previous motorcycle entitlement or when riding a moped
- already hold a full licence for another category in A.

When you've completed CBT you'll be given a DL196. Keep this safe. You must have a DL196 before you can take the practical motorcycle test.

CBT may be taken on a Direct Access motorcycle. Some of the initial parts however, may be covered around a standard learner machine.

CBT Certificates (DL196)

From 1 February 2001 CBT may be completed on

- a moped or motorcycle
- a motorcycle-sidecar combination or moped that has more than two wheels.

The DL196 will record whether CBT was completed on a two wheeled machine or one with more than two wheels and will validate provisional entitlement accordingly.

Certificate life   From 1 February 2001 CBT certificates have a two-year life:

- Certificates issued before that date will remain valid for the remainder of their three year life.
- A certificate validating full moped entitlement on a full car licence will remain valid for mopeds, for the life of the licence.

Note

If training is completed on a motorcycle-sidecar combination or on a moped that has more than two wheels

- moped validation will be limited to mopeds with more than two wheels
- motorcycle validation will be limited to motorcycle-sidecar combinations.

Foreign licence holders

Visitors or new residents

Visitors to Great Britain or new residents can drive on their foreign licence or International Driving Permit (IDP) for up to 12 months.

You must make sure that

- your licence or IDP is valid
- you have entitlement for the size of motorcycle you intend to ride
- you're aged 17 or over.

You must apply for a UK licence before riding if

- you don't have the correct motorcycle entitlement
- you've been in Great Britain for more than 12 months.

If you want to take a motorcycle test you'll have to hold a UK provisional licence or counterpart before you take

- the theory test
- the practical motorcycle test.

European Community and other driving licences

EC licences are valid for driving in the UK until they expire. Licences from designated countries can be exchanged for a UK licence within 12 months without the need to take a test.

If, however, your motorcycle entitlement was granted automatically when you passed a test in a car or other vehicle

- you'll be given full moped entitlement and provisional motorcycle entitlement
- you'll have to pass a motorcycle test to have full motorcycle entitlement.

Information Leaflet D100, 'What you need to know about driving licences' gives further information about foreign licences available for exchange.

This is available at larger Post Offices or you can get further advice from The Driver Enquiry Unit, The Driver and Vehicle Licensing Agency (DVLA), Swansea SA6 7JL.

Tel: 0870 240 0009

or

www.dvla.gov.uk/contact/dvlctact.htm#drivers.

How to obtain a full motorcycle licence (From 1 February 2001)

Type of licence currently held	CBT required?
Provisional driving licence	**Yes**, before you can ride on the road
Full car licence	**Yes**, before you can ride on the road
Full motorcycle licence (category A), and subject to the two-year qualifying period	**No**
Full motorcycle licence (sub-category A1)	**No**
Full moped licence, obtained by passing a moped test after 1 July 1996	**No**
Full moped licence, obtained by passing a moped test between 1 December 1990 and 1 July 1996	**No**
Full moped licence, obtained by passing a moped test before 1 December 1990	**Yes**, before you can ride a motorcycle on the road

How to obtain a full moped licence

Provisional moped licence (aged 16)	**Yes**, before you can ride on the road
Provisional driving licence	**Yes**, before you can ride on the road

How to validate full moped entitlement on a full car licence

Full car licence obtained by passing the driving test after 1 February 2001	**Yes.** DL196 remains valid for the life of the licence
Minimum test vehicles	**Engine**
Moped	Under 50 cc
Light motorcycle (A1)	75–125 cc
Standard motorcycle	121–125 cc
Accelerated access	Unspecified
Direct access	Unspecified

Theory test required?	Direct access	Accelerated access
Yes, before you take the practical test	Must be 21 or over	Not applicable
Yes, before you take the practical test	Must be 21 or over	Not applicable
No	Not applicable	Available if you're aged 21 or over
No	Must be 21 or over	Not applicable
No	Must be 21 or over	Not applicable
Yes, before you take the practical test	Must be 21 or over	Not applicable
Yes, before you take the practical test	Must be 21 or over	Not applicable
Yes, before you take the practical **moped** test	Not applicable	Not applicable
Yes, before you take the practical **moped** test	Not applicable	Not applicable

issued after 1 February 2001

No	Not applicable	Not applicable

Power	Speed
	50 kph (31 mph) max. (and doesn't weigh more than 250 kg)
11 kW (14.6 bhp) max.	If between 121–125 cc and can exceed 100 kph (62.5 mph) a category A will be given
11 kW (14.6 bhp) max.	Capable of exceeding 100 kph (62.5 mph)
35 kW (46.6 bhp) min.	Unspecified
35 kW (46.6 bhp) min.	Unspecified

Disqualified riders

Tough penalties exist for anyone convicted of dangerous riding or driving.

Courts will impose an extended test on anyone convicted of dangerous driving offences. They can also impose an extended test on anyone convicted of other offences involving obligatory disqualification.

If you've been disqualified for other endorsable offences the courts can order a normal-length test before you can recover a full licence.

Recovering a full licence

A rider subject to a retest can apply for a provisional licence at the end of the disqualification period. The normal rules for provisional licence holders will apply.

The theory test must be passed before applying for either an extended or a normal-length test.

CBT

If you have been disqualified your DL196 is rendered invalid by the disqualification, and CBT will have to be retaken.

The extended test

The extended motorcycle or moped test involves over 60 minutes' riding time. The test routes cover a wide variety of roads, usually including dual carriageways.

A rider has to

* maintain a satisfactory standard throughout the extended test period
* cope with a wide range of road and traffic conditions.

The examiner will apply the same standard of assessment as for an ordinary test. However, the extra time and wide variety of road and traffic conditions make the extended test more demanding. Candidates should make sure that they're well prepared before applying.

Higher fees

The higher fee for the extended motorcycle test reflects the extra length of the test.

New Drivers Act

How you may be affected

Special rules apply for the first two years after the date of passing your first practical test.

Your licence will be revoked if the number of penalty points on your licence reaches six or more as a result of offences you commit before the two years are over. This includes offences you committed before passing your test.

You must then reapply for a provisional licence. CBT will have to be completed again and all learner restrictions will apply until you pass the theory and practical test again.

This applies even if you pay by fixed penalty.

Vehicle documents

The registration document (VRD)

This contains details of your motorcycle

- make and model
- year of first registration
- engine size and number.

It also gives your name and address.

If you buy a new motorcycle the dealer will register it with DVLA. A registration document will then be sent directly to you from DVLA.

If you buy a second-hand machine you'll receive the VRD from the previous owner. Fill in the 'Change of ownership' section and send it off to DVLA at the address given on the document. You should do this immediately as it's an offence not to notify DVLA.

Vehicle excise duty

This is often called 'road tax' or the 'vehicle licence'. You must display the vehicle excise licence ('tax disc') on the vehicle.

Applying You can get the vehicle licence application form at any Post Office. Follow the instructions on the form. Most main Post Offices can accept your application.

The fee This varies with engine size.

These classes are

- up to 150 cc
- 151–250 cc
- over 250 cc.

Documents When you apply to renew your vehicle excise licence you must produce

- a vehicle test certificate (MOT) if your motorcycle is three years old and over
- a valid certificate of insurance
- an excise licence renewal form.

Older motorcycles Older motorcycles may be classed as 'historic' and as such are exempt from vehicle excise duty. If you have an older motorcycle check with DVLA to find out if it qualifies. Remember, all motorcycles must display a valid tax disc, even if no fee is payable.

The vehicle test certificate (MOT)

The MOT test applies to all motorcycles, mopeds and scooters over three years old. The test must be carried out every year at an appointed vehicle testing station. For motorcycles this is often, but not always, a motorcycle dealer.

Purpose of the test   The test is to check that your motorcycle is roadworthy at the time it's tested.

It's always the rider's responsibility to ensure that

- any fault which develops is promptly corrected
- any machine you're riding is roadworthy.

When your machine passes the test you'll be given a vehicle test certificate. You'll need to produce this document when you renew your vehicle excise licence.

If your motorcycle fails you must not ride it on the road unless you're taking it

- to have the failure faults corrected
- by prior appointment for a retest at the vehicle testing station.

When to test   You can have your motorcycle tested

- up to one month before it's three years old
- up to one month before the current certificate runs out. If you do this your new certificate will expire one year after the expiry date of the old one.

Insurance

It's illegal to ride without insurance. Should you cause injury to anyone or damage property it could result in prosecution.

Before you take a motorcycle onto public roads get proper insurance cover. You can arrange this through

- the insurance company directly
- a broker
- a motorcycle dealer
- the manufacturer (sometimes)
- the Internet.

The insurance company Insuring directly with an insurance company is probably a little cheaper than the same policy through a broker. Finding the best deal, however, can be a time consuming business.

A broker Many brokers are linked by computer to the main insurance companies. This allows them to get comparative quotes very quickly. A good broker will shop around and find the best policy for you.

If you already have car insurance ask your present insurer first.

A motorcycle dealer A dealer can act as a broker or may have a direct link with an insurance company. Sometimes the dealer can offer insurance deals through the manufacturers.

The manufacturer Some larger manufacturers make arrangements with insurance companies. This benefits the motorcyclist by offering competitive rates. Your dealer will be able to tell you about cover in this category.

Types of insurance

Third party This type of insurance is the legal minimum and the cheapest cover.

The 'third party' is any person you might injure or property you might damage. You aren't covered for damage to your motorcycle or injury to yourself.

If you damage another vehicle the owner could claim against your insurance. On the other hand, if someone damaged your motorcycle you could claim against them.

Third party fire and theft This is the same as third party but it also covers you for

- your motorcycle being stolen
- damage by fire.

Comprehensive This is the best, but the most expensive insurance. Apart from covering other persons and property from injury and damage this also covers damage to your machine.

Pillion passenger insurance All policies include cover for a pillion passenger. This is much the same as for car passengers.

The cost of insurance

This varies with

- your age – the younger you are, the more it will cost
- the make of your motorcycle
- the power and capacity of the engine
- where you live.

Engine-size groups for insurance purposes can vary from one insurer to another. This is another reason to shop around when looking for insurance cover.

What's insured

This also varies from company to company. Read the small print and ask your insurer or broker.

You'll often have to pay the first £50 or £100 of any claim. This is called the 'excess'.

Shop around and buy the best policy you can afford.

The certificate of insurance

This is a short and simple document which certifies

- who is insured
- the type of vehicle covered
- the kind of insurance cover
- the period of cover
- the main conditions.

Sometimes a broker will give you a temporary certificate or 'cover note'. This is issued while you're waiting for your certificate and is proof of insurance.

Keep the certificate safe and produce it

- if the police ask you
- when you apply to renew your vehicle excise licence.

The policy document

This contains the full details of the contract between you and the insurance company. It's usually written in legal language. Ask your broker or the insurance company to explain any details which you don't understand.

Motorcycles come in many different types and sizes. You need to think carefully before deciding which one to buy. Buying one that doesn't suit your needs can be a costly mistake and could spoil your enjoyment of motorcycling.

Apart from buying the machine you'll have to consider

- insurance
- running costs
- clothing.

This part looks at what you need to consider when buying a motorcycle. It also describes the various types of motorcycle and their main features.

The topics covered

- buying a motorcycle
- mopeds
- learner motorcycles
- automatic motorcycles
- commuter motorcycles
- sports motorcycles
- touring motorcycles
- custom motorcycles
- off-road motorcycles (trail bikes).

Buying a motorcycle

When you're thinking about buying a motorcycle you need to consider

- your budget
- the type of motorcycle you would like
- the location of the nearest dealer.

You'll also want to know where to get advice if you need it.

Budget

Costs you'll have to think about include

- **purchase price** This may determine whether you buy new or second-hand
- **insurance** Some models cost a lot more to insure than others
- **running costs** Fuel consumption, tyres and the cost of spare parts need to be considered
- **clothing** If you're new to motorcycling the cost of a helmet, gloves, jacket, boots, etc. can be a major consideration.

Type of motorcycle

When choosing a machine you'll need to ask yourself about

- **your licence** Are you entitled to ride motorcycles of any engine size?
- **suitability** What do you want from your motorcycle? A commuter machine is going to struggle with long-distance motorway riding
- **comfort** Are you comfortable on the machine? Can you reach the controls easily? Can your feet reach the ground?
- **weight** Some motorcycles are very heavy. This can present problems when parking or manoeuvring.

Motorcycle dealers

The motorcycle dealership in your area could influence your decision. Being able to have your machine serviced locally could be important to you. A dealer can also

- offer finance packages
- offer part exchange deals
- offer special insurance rates
- arrange training courses
- let you try out a motorcycle before you make a final decision (subject to your licence entitlement)
- give you expert advice.

Further information

You can get further information from manufacturers' brochures, magazines and newspapers. Talking to other riders can give you another viewpoint. However, at the end of the day, the final choice is always yours.

Mopeds

A moped is a motorcycle which

- must not have an engine over 50 cc
- can't go faster than 50 kph (31 mph)
- doesn't weigh more than 250 kg
- can be moved by pedals, if the moped was registered before 1 August 1977.

A moped can be ridden without L-plates (or D-plates in Wales) by people who hold a full car, moped or motorcycle licence. Full car licence holders who passed their test on or after 1 February 2001 must complete CBT to validate their full moped entitlement. (See Part two)

Learner motorcycles

These motorcycles are suitable for use by learners provided

- the engine isn't over 125 cc
- the engine power output doesn't exceed 11 kW (14.6 bhp)
- L-plates (or D-plates in Wales) are fitted both to the front and back of the machine.

(These engine size restrictions don't apply to learners under the accelerated or direct access schemes. See Part two.)

Automatic motorcycles

Automatic or semi-automatic motorcycles
have automatic transmission. They're usually
small and easy to ride. You can take your
motorcycle test on one of these machines.
If you pass your full licence entitlement
will be restricted to such machines.

Automatic motorcycles are ideal for
short trips and for use in heavy
town traffic.

Commuter motorcycles

Commuter machines are especially suitable
for shorter journeys. They're

• economical to run
• lightweight and easy to ride
• low powered
• available with automatic, semi-automatic
  and manual transmissions.

Sports motorcycles

These motorcycles have road racing styling. They come in a variety of engine sizes and can be

- expensive to buy and run
- capable of very high speed.

When you ride this type of machine for the first time, take care. You may find yourself going faster than you intended.

Touring motorcycles

Touring motorcycles are designed for comfortable long distance riding. They feature

- a relaxed riding position
- luggage carrying capacity
- often some form of fairing for weather protection
- a large engine.

Despite their size and weight these motorcycles are capable of continuous travel at motorway speeds.

Custom motorcycles

Sometimes called 'cruisers', these motorcycles are recognisable by their unique styling. They

- are available in a wide range of engine sizes, including 125 cc
- usually have a low seat height
- have a 'laid back' riding position.

Off-road motorcycles (trail bikes)

Trail bikes are designed so that they can be used both on and off the road. This type of motorcycle

- comes in a wide range of engine sizes
- has extra ground clearance, which increases the seat height
- is fitted with dual purpose tyres
- is built to cope with riding over rough ground.

Without the right clothing you can get very cold and wet when riding a motorcycle. Special motorcycling clothing is available which

- protects you from the weather
- helps to protect you from some types of injury
- helps other road users to see you.

The topics covered

- visors and goggles
- safety helmets
- protective clothing
- gloves and gauntlets
- boots
- visibility aids
- motorcycle fairings
- windscreens
- handlebar muffs.

CLOTHING AND WEATHER PROTECTION

Visors and goggles

A visor or goggles are vital to protect your eyes from wind, rain, insects and road dirt.

All visors and goggles must

- comply with British Standard
  - BS 4110 Grade X, or
  - BS 4110 Grade XA, or
  - BS 4110 Grade YA, or
  - BS 4110 Grade ZA

and

- display a BSI kitemark

or

- comply with a European standard which offers a level of safety and protection at least equivalent to these British Standards and carry a mark equivalent to the BSI kitemark (ECE 22-05).

Goggles may comply with the EU Directive on Personal Protective Equipment and carry the 'CE' mark.

Glasses and tinted eyewear

If you normally wear glasses or contact lenses you must by law wear them when you ride.

Don't wear tinted glasses, visors or goggles if you're riding in

- the dark
- conditions of poor visibility.

Cleaning your visor or goggles

It's very important that you keep your visor or goggles clean. You must have a clear view of the road ahead at all times.

To clean your goggles or visor wash them in warm soapy water. Don't use solvents or petrol.

In cold and wet weather your visor or goggles might fog up on the inside. You can use a special anti-fog spray to help prevent this. If your visor or goggles fog up when you're riding

- choose somewhere safe to stop
- wipe them with a clean damp cloth. Carry a cloth with you for this purpose.

Damaged or scratched goggles and visors

Scratches on your visor or goggles can

- distort your view
- cause dazzle from the lights of oncoming vehicles at night
- cause glare, especially from low winter sun.

If your visor or goggles are heavily scratched renew them.

DSA MOTORCYCLE RIDING   33

Safety helmets

By law, you must wear a safety helmet when riding a motorcycle on the road (members of the Sikh religion who wear a turban are exempt).

All helmets sold in the UK must either

- comply with British Standard BS 6658: 1985 and carry the BSI kitemark, or
- comply with UNECE Regulation 22.05 (it will be marked with a UN 'E' mark - the first two digits of the approval number will be '05'), or
- comply with any standard accepted by a member of the European Economic Area (EEA State) which offers a level of safety and protection equivalent to BS 6658: 1985 and carry a mark equivalent to the BSI kitemark.

Types of safety helmet

Motorcycle helmets are either

- full-face, or
- open-face.

Full-face helmets   This type of helmet

- covers the head fully and has a hinged visor
- protects the face in an accident

- offers more weather protection than an open-face helmet.

Open-face helmets   This type of helmet

- is preferred by riders who feel closed in by full-face helmets
- can be worn with either a visor or goggles
- doesn't protect the chin in an accident.

Whichever type of helmet you choose, you must make sure that it

- fits properly
- is correctly fastened.

Helmet fit

When you buy a new helmet make sure that it's a good, firm fit. The padding will soon bed down and this could make the helmet loose. A loose helmet isn't only uncomfortable, it could also come off in an accident.

Helmet fastening

The three different helmet fastening methods in use today are illustrated.

Some helmet straps also have a velcro tab to secure the strap so that it doesn't flap in the wind. It **isn't** to be used to fasten the helmet.

It is both unsafe and illegal to ride in a helmet which isn't

- fastened correctly
- fastened at all.

Double D-ring

Quick release

Bar and buckle

Helmet materials

The outer shell of motorcycle safety helmets are made in three basic materials

- polycarbonate
- glass fibre
- kevlar.

Each material has its own characteristics.

Polycarbonate

- lighter than glass fibre
- must not be painted or have stickers affixed
- must not be cleaned with solvents.

Polycarbonate helmets tend to be cheaper than other types and don't last as long.

Glass fibre

- heavier than polycarbonate
- lasts longer than polycarbonate
- easy to clean.

Kevlar

- extremely tough
- used as a composite with glass fibre, or carbon and glass fibre
- combines great strength with light weight
- tends to be expensive.

Damage to helmets

If your helmet receives any serious impact buy a new one. Damage won't always be visible to the naked eye. For this reason never use a second-hand helmet. A damaged helmet could be unreliable in an accident. Repairs to damaged helmets are not recommended.

Protective clothing

Clothing is available which will keep you warm and dry in all but the worst conditions. If you allow yourself to become cold and wet when riding you'll lose concentration.

Protective clothing for motorcyclists is designed to protect you from

- the cold and wet
- some kinds of injury.

Clothing for which a manufacturer either claims or implies protection, other than from the weather, must be marked with the 'CE' mark.

Motorcycle protective clothing is of two main types

- clothing made from man-made materials
- leather clothing.

Man-made materials

To protect you from the weather, nylon is the most popular material. It's available in many different forms and comes under many different brand names. Other materials such as waxed cotton and PVC are also available.

More expensive garments have reinforcing and padding at the shoulders and elbows. This provides some protection in the event of an accident.

Generally, man-made outer clothing is designed to fit over your normal clothes and comes as

- a jacket and trousers
- a one-piece suit
- lined or unlined.

  When you're buying outer clothing make sure that

  - you have enough room for extra layers of warm clothing underneath
  - your movement isn't restricted.

Leathers

Motorcyclists have traditionally worn leathers. They offer a high degree of protection from gravel burns if you fall off. Motorcycle leathers come as

- one-piece suits
- two-piece zip-together suits
- separate jacket and trousers
- lined or unlined.

One-piece suits Leather motorcycle suits aren't designed to fit over your normal clothes. They do, however, offer the motorcyclist certain advantages

- reduced wind resistance
- a high degree of windproofing.

They also have some disadvantages

- expensive to buy
- only showerproof. You'll have to use a waterproof oversuit in wet weather
- not warm. Due to the close fit, you can't wear extra layers underneath in cold weather
- there can be some restriction of movement.

Two piece nip together suits These comprise a separate jacket and trousers which zip together. This style has some advantages:

- you can buy the jacket or trousers separately. This lets you spread the cost to suit your budget. It also lets you buy different sizes to suit you
- zipping the jacket and trousers together helps to stop draughts around your waist
- jacket or trousers can be worn separately.

Separate jacket and trousers This option

- is often the least expensive
- gives you a wide choice of styles, colours, sizes and prices.

When you are choosing leathers look for additional protection for shoulders, elbows and knees.

Visit your motorcycle dealer or motorcycle clothing supplier. Try on various types of clothing for fit and comfort. As a general rule, buy the best you can afford.

Gloves and gauntlets

Good gloves or gauntlets are essential when you ride a motorcycle. Never be tempted to ride without gloves. If you fall off you could seriously injure your hands. Your gloves should

- protect your hands from cold and wet weather
- protect your hands if you fall off
- allow you to operate the controls easily.

Gauntlets prevent wind and rain from being driven up your sleeves. However, in heavy rain the water can sometimes run down your sleeves into your gloves. Modern motorcycle gauntlets have adjustable cuffs to help overcome this problem.

Materials

Leather is the most suitable material for motorcycle gloves. On its own it's tough, supple and resistant to water, but when combined with modern materials and construction methods it can be used to make waterproof gloves. Gloves made from cheaper materials don't provide the same level of protection. For protection from prolonged rain you may need to wear overmitts.

Overmitts

Overmitts prevent gloves from becoming sodden in prolonged wet weather riding. You wear them over your usual motorcycle gloves or gauntlets. They are made from waterproof material, either waxed cotton or nylon. Make sure that you can operate the controls properly when wearing overmitts.

Cold

When riding in very cold weather your hands can become painfully cold. No matter how good your gloves, the cold will eventually get through. This in turn can cause you to lose concentration when riding.

To overcome the cold you can try wearing thin inner gloves. Experiment with various combinations to find one that suits you.

Heated gloves and handlebar grips

If you're serious about motorcycling in cold weather then you'll need either

- electrically heated inner gloves
- electrically heated handlebar grips.

These accessories put a large demand on your motorcycle's electrical generator. Check that it can cope with the extra demands before you buy and fit them.

Boots

It's important to wear good boots or stout footwear when you ride a motorcycle. If you wear sandals or trainers your feet will have little protection if you fall off.

Motorcycle boots

- protect your feet from cold and wet weather
- offer some protection if you have an accident
- protect your feet and shins from knocks and bumps.

Types of boots

There are three types of motorcycle boots

- leather
- rubber
- plastic.

Leather boots Leather is strong, flexible and weather resistant. This makes it the most suitable material for motorcycle boots. Leather boots give the best protection in the event of an accident.

Boots made from leather combined with modern materials and construction techniques can resist water, even in the wettest conditions. However, leather alone isn't totally waterproof and you might need to wear overboots in very wet weather.

Leather boots are available either unlined or lined with warm fleece material.

Rubber or plastic boots Rubber or plastic boots are

- waterproof
- cheaper than leather.

You can buy them lined or unlined, and leather-look boots are also available.

Whichever type of boot you decide to buy make sure that

- they're comfortable
- you can operate the foot controls easily.

Try as many different boots as you can. Always buy the best you can afford.

Cold

Your feet can become very cold when you're riding in wintry conditions. Wearing an extra pair of socks can help. If your feet become too cold stop and warm up before continuing your journey.

Fluorescent
jacket

In daylight

Wearing fluorescent orange or yellow clothing will improve your chances of being seen. This can be

- a fluorescent jacket
- a fluorescent tabard or waistcoat
- a 'Sam Browne' belt.

You need to be visible from the side as well as the front and back.

Other methods you could use to help other road users to see you in daylight include

- wearing a white helmet
- wearing brightly coloured clothing
- riding with your headlamp on dipped beam.

Visibility aids

Many road accidents involving motorcyclists occur because another road user didn't see them. Using some form of visibility aid will help others to see you.

In the dark

To improve visibility in the dark you need to wear reflective material. This can be reflective

- belts
- patches
- strips.

They work by reflecting the light from headlamps of other vehicles. This makes you much more visible from a long distance away.

Reflective strips on your gloves will help other road users to see your arm signals.

Reflective strips

Reflective patches

Motorcycle fairings

Motorcycle fairings come in three main types

- handlebar fairings.
- touring fairings
- sports fairings

Handlebar fairings

These protect your hands and body and are available in either sports or touring styles.

Touring fairings

These provide weather protection to the hands, legs and feet. They also make high-speed riding more comfortable by keeping you out of the wind.

Sports fairings

These give some weather protection but they're mainly intended to cut down wind resistance.

WIndscreens

These protect your face and body from the wind and rain.

Handlebar muffs

Handlebar muffs are designed to keep the wind and rain off your hands.

Motorcycles have various types of controls. Before you learn to ride you should become familiar with their position, function and use.

Most motorcycles have the controls in similar positions but there are some important differences. For example, most motorcycles have manual transmission but some have automatic and others semi-automatic.

This part is a general guide to the controls on a typical motorcycle.

The topics covered

- typical position of controls
- left handlebar controls
- right handlebar controls
- mirrors
- foot controls
- anti-lock braking systems (ABS)
- traction control system (TCS)
- linked braking sytems
- instrument panel.

Typical position of controls

Mirrors

Ignition switch

Clutch lever

Left handlebar
control switches

Fuel tap detail

Gear selector

Instrument panel

Front brake lever

Throttle

Right handlebar
control switches

Rear brake pedal

Kick starter

ON
OFF
FUEL
RES

Left handlebar controls

Headlamp dip switch

Lets you switch your headlamp between main beam and dipped beam.

On main beam you'll usually see a blue warning lamp on your instruments. At night, switch to dipped beam when meeting or following other vehicles. This will stop you dazzling other drivers.

Headlamp flasher

This switch lets you flash your headlamp. This has the same meaning as sounding your horn. Flash your headlamp if your horn may not be heard, for example on the motorway.

Clutch lever

Choke

Horn

Sound the horn to warn other road users if you don't think they've seen you.

You must not sound your horn

- between 11.30 pm and 7 am in a built-up area
- when your motorcycle is stationary, unless a moving vehicle poses a danger.

Indicators

You use the indicators to let other road users know that you intend to change direction. You must make sure that you cancel them after turning.

Clutch lever

Operates the clutch, which engages and disengages the engine from the drive to the rear wheel.

Use the clutch

- when you select first gear before moving off
- to prevent the engine stalling when you stop
- to help change gears
- when selecting neutral.

To change or select a gear

- pull the clutch lever fully to the handlebar
- select the gear you need
- release the clutch lever smoothly to engage the clutch.

Fully automatic motorcycles This type of motorcycle has no clutch lever. You select drive or neutral as required. Often the rear brake lever is fitted in place of the clutch lever.

Semi-automatic motorcycles These have no clutch lever. The clutch operates automatically when you use the gear-change pedal.

Choke

A device which helps when starting a cold engine. It operates by changing the amount of air in the air/fuel mixture which the engine burns.

When you're starting a cold engine

- move the choke control to 'on'
- start the engine
- gradually move the choke control to 'off' as the engine warms up.

Note Failure to return the choke to 'off' could cause the engine to run faster than normal. This could make it difficult to control the motorcycle, especially when slowing down. In addition it could cause excessive wear to the engine and excessive fuel consumption.

Right handlebar controls

Engine cut-out switch

This is to stop the engine in an emergency.

When stopping the engine normally, use the ignition switch. You're less likely to leave your keys in the ignition when leaving your motorcycle.

Electric starter

This is fitted as well as, or in place of, the kick starter.

Use

- check the cut-out switch is on.
- switch the ignition on.
- make sure that the gear selector is in neutral.
- press the starter button.

Light switch

A three-position switch letting you select

- headlights
- parking lights
- off.

Front brake lever

Applies the brake to the front wheel. (unless part of the linked braking system. See 'linked braking systems' later in this part).

To apply the front brake squeeze the lever toward you. Use all the fingers on your right hand for maximum control and stopping power. The harder you squeeze, the harder you brake. To release the brake, release the lever.

Throttle

The throttle controls the engine speed. It increases or decreases the amount of fuel delivered to the engine.

To speed up the engine twist the throttle towards you. To slow down the engine twist the grip away from you. Most throttles will spring back to a closed position when released. In this position the engine should run at 'idle' or 'tick over' speed.

Mirrors

Fitted to both right and left handlebars, or sometimes on the fairing.

Mirrors should be adjusted to give you the best view of the road behind. However, your elbows may obscure the view behind. If they do, try fitting mirrors with longer stems.

There are two types of mirror available:

- **flat mirrors** These don't distort the picture of the road behind. This makes it easier for you to judge the speed and distance of following traffic
- **convex mirrors** These are slightly curved and give a wider field of vision. This makes it more difficult to judge the speed and distance of following traffic

Foot controls

Gear selector

Gears enable you to match engine power to road speed. Low gears allow the engine power to be used at lower road speeds. Use these when you're moving off, going uphill or accelerating. High gears allow the same engine power to be used at higher road speeds.

Changing smoothly through the gears is a skill that improves with practice.

Position The gear selector is usually on the left side of the motorcycle. It's just in front of the footrest.

Some mopeds and scooters have a twist-grip gear change on the left handlebar.

Neutral The neutral position is when no gear is engaged. Most motorcycles have a green warning lamp to show when the gears are in neutral.

Gear selector __ neutral position

To select gears On motorcycles the gears are selected by lifting or pushing down the gear lever with your foot. The positions and number of gears vary with the make of motorcycle.

Rear brake pedal

This applies the brake to the rear wheel (unless part of the linked braking system. See 'Linked braking systems' later in this part).

Position This pedal is usually on the right side of the motorcycle, just in front of the footrest. Some automatic motorcycles have the rear brake lever on the left handlebar.

Use To apply the brake press the pedal with your foot. To release the brake release the pedal.

Kick-start lever

Position Usually found on the right side of the motorcycle, near the footrest.

Use

- make sure that the cut-out switch is on
- switch on the ignition
- put the gear selector in neutral and check that the neutral lamp glows
- fold out the kick-start lever, (you may need to fold the footrest out of the way)
- tread down sharply on the lever. Repeat this until the engine starts.

Anti-lock braking systems (ABS)

Anti-lock braking systems are designed to prevent wheel lock caused by excessive braking. This can enable the rider to achieve maximum braking when travelling in a straight line.

ABS cannot increase tyre grip or prevent skids where other factors are at work such as when cornering.

Wheel speed sensors detect when a wheel is beginning to lock. The system releases the braking pressure just enough to prevent wheel lock. The sensor monitors wheel movement hundreds of times per second and will keep the wheel at the point of lock-up

• for as long as the rider continues to brake hard enough to activate the system

or

• until the motorcycle is stopped.

You should refer to the owner's handbook for details of the manufacturer's recommended method of use.

Remember

ABS cannot overcome the laws of physics. It will still be possible to skid because poor riding has failed to take account of the road conditions. ABS is a safety aid designed to enhance your skills, NOT replace them.

ABS warning lamp

Anti-lock braking systems will have a warning lamp. Generally it will light up when you turn on the ignition and may not go out until the motorcycle is travelling at 5-10 mph.

Read your owner's manual to find out how the system is designed to operate on your motorcycle.

Traction control system (TCS)

Traction control systems help prevent wheelspin when accelerating. This is most likely to occur on slippery surfaces. A sensor detects the rear wheel starting to spin and the system adjusts the power driving the rear wheel so that grip is maintained.

A warning lamp may show to signal when TCS is in operation.

TCS may also be activated by riding over a sudden change in road level - such as a hump backed bridge.

While TCS enables a rider to make maximum use of the tyres' grip during acceleration, it cannot prevent loss of grip caused by cornering too fast or failing to take account of road and weather conditions.

Linked braking sytems

Some motorcycles have a linked braking system where use of one brake control activates both brakes.

If your motorcycle has a linked brake system fitted refer to your owner's manual for the manufacturer's recommendations on their use. However, full braking effectiveness will be achieved by applying both brakes together.

Instrument panel

Speedometer

Tells you how fast you're going in miles per hour and kilometres per hour.

Temperature gauge

Fitted to motorcycles with liquid cooled engines. It shows the coolant temperature and warns if the engine is overheating.

Mileometer (odometer)

Usually housed in the speedometer. It shows an overall total of how many miles or kilometres your motorcycle has covered.

Ignition switch

Operated by the ignition key. There are four positions:

- off
- on
- lock. In this position the steering locks to help prevent theft
- 'P' for Park. Used for parking at night when the parking lamp is required.

Rev. counter

Shows the engine speed in revolutions ('revs') per minute.

Ignition lamp

Comes on when you switch on the ignition. It should go out when the engine is running. If it doesn't, this shows a problem with the battery charging system.

Neutral lamp

Glows to tell you when the gear selector is in the neutral position.

High beam lamp

Indicates when your headlamp is on high beam.

Oil pressure lamp

Warns you of low oil pressure. If it comes on when the engine is running, you may have a serious problem. Stop the engine immediately and investigate the cause.

Indicator repeater

Tells you that your indicators are in use. Use it to check if you've cancelled a signal.

This part takes you through the basics of motorcycle handling and control. Before you ride on busy roads and in traffic, you must have full control of your motorcycle at all times, and this involves

- a good working knowledge of the various controls
- being able to coordinate hand and foot controls together.

The topics covered

- getting started
- stands
- mounting and dismounting
- riding position
- starting the engine
- moving off
- using the brakes
- stopping safely
- emergency braking
- using the gears
- signals
- moving off at an angle
- moving off uphill
- stopping the engine.

In addition you need to have

- an understanding of the rules of the road
- a respect for the needs of other road users
- a basic knowledge to enable you to check to make sure everything is working correctly and the machine is safe before setting out.

Getting started

Starting to ride isn't just a matter of starting the engine and setting off.

You should first of all check your motorcycle to make sure it's safe and ready for the road.

Everyday checks

Make a habit of checking daily that

- all lights (including indicators) are working; replace any dead bulbs immediately (it's a good idea to carry spare fuses and bulbs).
- the brakes are working; **don't ride with faulty brakes**.
- the wheels and tyres show no sign of damage.

Periodic checks

These checks are both for safety and good vehicle maintenance.

Check and top up if necessary:

- engine oil
- water level in the radiator or expansion tank of liquid cooled engines
- brake fluid level
- battery: top up with distilled water if necessary (some batteries are maintenance free and don't need topping up).

You should also check tyres and make sure they are

- legal: they must have the correct tread depth and be free of dangerous cuts and defects
- at the right pressure.

How often?

How often you make the checks depends on how much you ride. Consult your motorcycle owner's handbook. If you ride a lot, you may need to do these every day.

Basic maintenance

Further information about basic maintenance can be found in Part fifteen of this manual.

Regular servicing

Have your motorcycle serviced regularly. The owner's handbook will tell you when servicing is recommended.

Stands

When you park a motorcycle you use a stand to support it. Motorcycles have either a centre or side stand, and many models are fitted with both.

Centre stand

The centre stand gives more stable support than the side stand. It also supports the motorcycle so that maintenance can be carried out such as

• drive chain adjustment (where fitted)

• wheel removal.

The centre stand needs to be used on a firm, level surface for maximum stability.

To put your motorcycle onto the centre stand

• position yourself on the left of the motorcycle, holding the left handlebar with the left hand

• push the stand down with your right foot (or left foot, if preferred) and hold the frame near the saddle with your right hand (some machines have a special handle).

• hold the stand down with your foot and pull the machine backwards and upwards.

To take your motorcycle off the centre stand

• position yourself on the left of the motorcycle. Put your left foot (or right, if preferred) in front of the centre stand

• hold the left handlebar with your left hand. Hold the frame near the saddle with your right hand

• pull the motorcycle forward. As it comes off the stand move your right hand to the front brake to keep control.

Warning

If the stand isn't fully up it could dig into the road when you're cornering and cause an accident.

Side stand

The side stand is generally quicker and easier to use than the centre stand. It relies on the motorcycle leaning over onto the stand for stability.

Care must be taken to ensure that

- the surface is firm enough to prevent the side stand sinking and the motorcycle falling over
- the slope of the ground doesn't prevent the motorcycle leaning onto the stand. If the machine is too upright it will be unstable.

To put your motorcycle onto the side stand:

- position yourself on the left of the machine, holding the left handlebar
- with the machine upright, push down the stand with your foot
- let the machine lean towards you until its weight is taken on the stand.

To take your motorcycle off the side stand:

- position yourself on the left of the machine holding the handlebars
- push the motorcycle upright
- move the stand to its 'up' position with your foot. Make sure it locks securely in position.

Warning

If the stand isn't fully up it could dig into the road when you're cornering and cause an accident. Some manufacturers fit a safety inhibitor switch to the side stand. Dependent upon the manufacturer, this prevents

- the engine being started while the side stand is down
- the engine running while the side stand is down
- the engine running if you try to ride off with the side stand down.

If your motorcycle

- refuses to start

or

- the engine cuts out when you select a gear

it could be that it is fitted with such a safety feature and you should be aware of its function.

Mounting and dismounting

Always mount from the left of the motorcycle, the side away from the traffic. As you get on or off apply the front brake to stop the motorcycle moving.

Practise mounting and dismounting with the motorcycle off its stand.

Balancing and wheeling your motorcycle

After you've practised mounting and dismounting, wheel the machine forward. Leaning the motorcycle towards you makes it easier to balance.

Work the front brake with your right hand to control the speed.

Practise wheeling the machine in circles, both to the left and to the right. Keep practising until you're able to balance and control it fully.

Adjusting the controls

You can adjust the main motorcycle controls to suit your individual needs. If you can't use them comfortably and safely when you're riding, adjust the

- hand controls, such as front brake and clutch levers
- foot controls, such as the footbrake and gear selector.

DSA MOTORCYCLE RIDING

Riding position

When you're seated on a stationary motorcycle you should be able to

- place both feet on the ground
- use one foot to keep your balance and the other to work the foot controls.

The best posture

Sit in a natural position, as determined by the machine design. You should be able to reach all the controls comfortably.

Starting the engine

Some engines can require a knack to make them start. The following is a general guide, but you may need to modify it to suit your machine.

To start the engine:

- make sure that the gear selector is in neutral. The neutral lamp on the instument panel will glow when the ignition is turned on. If no neutral lamp is fitted push your motorcycle forward to see if the rear wheel turns freely
- turn the fuel tap to 'on'
- if the engine is cold move the choke to 'on'
- make sure that the engine cut-out switch is in the 'on' position
- turn the ignition key to the 'on' position.

Your motorcycle is now ready to start. The next step depends on whether your machine has an electric starter or a kick starter.

Electric starter

- press the starter button
- as the engine starts, release the starter button and open the throttle to give a fairly high engine speed
- as the engine warms up move the choke to 'off'.

Kick starter

- fold out the kick-start lever. On some machines you'll have to fold the footrest up before you can use the kick starter
- place your instep on the lever and tread down sharply. Allow the kick-start lever to return to its upright position. Repeat this until the engine starts
- when the engine has started, fold the kick-start lever back to its resting position
- open the throttle to give a fairly high engine speed
- as the engine warms up move the choke to 'off'.

Moving off

To move off safely on the road you have to think about other road users. Can you move off without endangering yourself or anyone else? To answer this question you need to have a good look around.

To move off, follow these steps in order:

- sit astride your machine
- apply the front brake and then start the engine
- squeeze in the clutch lever. Use all your fingers to get full control
- select first gear. Keep the clutch lever held in
- put your left foot on the ground and shift the weight of the machine to that foot. Put your right foot on the footrest and then apply the rear brake.

Now look round over your right shoulder (unless you're on the right-hand side of the road) and then look ahead. You're looking to make sure that

- there's no traffic approaching from behind
- the way ahead is clear
- you're safe to move off.

Look out for pedestrians and cyclists – they're harder to see than cars.

You should signal if it will help any other road user.

Important It's very important that you look round before moving off, even if you have mirrors fitted. Looking round will allow you to

- judge accurately how far away any traffic may be, and how fast it's travelling

- see if there's anything in the blind area on your right. The blind area is the area behind and to your right which isn't covered by mirrors (see Part nine on 'Bends and junctions').

Clutch control

You can now release the front brake and work the throttle.

- release the clutch lever smoothly, until you feel the engine trying to move the machine. This is called the 'biting point'. You must be able to find the biting point easily when releasing the clutch lever. This skill will develop with practice. Open the throttle enough to keep the engine running smoothly
- gradually release the clutch lever and at the same time open the throttle smoothly. As you move off release the rear brake and bring your left foot up onto the footrest.

Smooth clutch control is essential to good riding. It's also one of the most difficult skills for the novice to acquire.

Balance

When you're manoeuvring a motorcycle the weight may make it awkward to handle. When you're riding, however, you should find the weight improves the stability and balance.

Never look down at the front wheel when riding – this can severely upset your balance.

Using the brakes

How to brake

Many motorcycle riders are, quite wrongly, afraid to use the front brake. This is often as a result of what they were taught as cyclists. On a motorcycle

- you must normally use both brakes
- the front brake is the more powerful of the two brakes and the most important when stopping a motorcycle.

To stop most effectively

In good road and weather conditions

- apply the front brake just before you apply the rear brake
- apply greater pressure to the front brake.

Applying greater pressure to the front brake gives the best stopping power in good conditions because

- the combined weight of the machine and rider is thrown forward
- the front tyre is pressed more firmly on the road, giving a better grip.

In wet or slippery conditions you need to apply a more equal pressure to both front and rear brakes.

Using one brake only   You'll take much longer to stop by using one brake only. But at very low speeds (walking pace) using only the rear brake gives smoother control.

Front brakes only applied

Rear brakes only applied

Both brakes applied

DSA MOTORCYCLE RIDING

When to brake

Always look and plan well ahead to avoid having to brake sharply. A gradual increase of pressure on the brakes is better than late, harsh braking.

Follow these rules:

- brake when your machine is upright and moving in a straight line
- brake in good time
- adjust the pressure on the brakes according to the road surface and weather conditions.

Where to brake

Where you brake is very important. The best time to brake is when you're travelling

- upright
- in a straight line.

Braking on a bend

A good rider will plan well ahead to avoid braking on a bend. On a bend the combined weight of motorcycle and rider is thrown outwards. To balance this the rider leans inwards.

If you brake on a bend

- the weight will be thrown outwards even more
- the motorcycle and rider may become unstable
- the tyres may lose their grip on the road surface.

If you must brake on a bend

- avoid using the front brake. Rely on the rear brake and engine braking to slow you down. If you must use the front brake, be very gentle. There's a risk of the front tyre losing its grip and sliding sideways
- try to bring your motorcycle upright and brake normally, provided you can do so safely.

Stopping safely

To stop safely you need to make sure that you don't endanger any other road users. You should

- use your mirrors and look over your right shoulder, if necessary, to check for following traffic
- signal if it will help other road users. People in front may benefit from a signal just as much as people behind.

Stopping

The following sequence will apply to most motorcycles:

- close the throttle
- apply both brakes smoothly until the machine stops
- just before the motorcycle stops pull in the clutch lever to avoid stalling the engine
- as the machine stops put your left foot on the ground to support the weight.

When the machine has stopped

- keep the front brake applied
- release the rear brake and support the motorcycle with your right foot.

With the clutch lever still pulled in

- use your left foot to move the gear selector to neutral
- release the clutch lever
- place both feet on the ground.

Disengaging the clutch

When stopping from very low speeds pull in the clutch lever **just before** or **just as** you brake.

When stopping from higher speeds always brake first, then pull in the clutch lever just before you stop.

Emergency braking

If you plan ahead you should seldom need to brake violently or stop suddenly. Nevertheless, emergencies do arise and you must be able to stop safely and quickly.

Maximum braking

- use the front brake just before the rear
- brake progressively (increase pressure steadily)
- apply the right amount of braking effort to each wheel. This will depend on the road surface and weather conditions.

Braking in an emergency

- keep your motorcycle upright
- apply maximum effort without locking the wheels. This is achieved by progressively increasing braking pressure. Don't use the brakes violently – this may cause you to skid
- pull in the clutch lever just before you stop.

Signalling when you brake

Don't try to give an arm signal when you brake in an emergency because

- you'll need both hands on the handlebars
- your stop lamp will warn traffic behind you.

Rear brakes only

Front brakes only

Both brakes applied (front first)

These three bikes were travelling at 40 mph before braking together.

Using the gears

Gear changing

To change up or down through
the gears you need to be able to co-ordinate
the

- clutch
- throttle
- gear selector.

Gear
selector
neutral
and
return
position

Changing up Change gear when you've
reached the appropriate speed for the next
gear.

- simultaneously close the throttle and pull
  in the clutch lever
- select the next higher gear by lifting the
  gear selector with the toe of your boot
  Allow the selector to return to its normal
  position after each change
- release the clutch lever smoothly and
  open the throttle at the same time
- repeat the sequence for each upward gear
  change.

Always travel in the highest suitable gear.
You'll save fuel and spare your engine.

Changing down

- simultaneously close the throttle and pull
  in the clutch lever
- select the next lower gear by pushing
  down the gear selector with the toe of
  your boot. Allow the selector to return to
  its normal position after each gear change
- at the same time, release the clutch lever
  smoothly and open the throttle as
  necessary.

When to change

Experience will tell you when to change gear.
You'll be able to hear from the engine sound
when a gear change is needed. Never let the
engine

- race when you could change to a
  higher gear
- labour when you could change to a
  lower gear.

Signals

You need to give signals to

- help other road users, including pedestrians
- let other road users know what you intend to do.

Road users include

- drivers of following and oncoming vehicles
- cyclists
- pedestrians
- traffic controllers
- police directing traffic.

Always signal **clearly** and in **good time**. Give only correct signals, as shown.

Arm signals

Arm signals are very effective in daylight especially when you're wearing bright or fluorescent clothing.

Giving an arm signal means that you have reduced steering control, if only briefly. Spend some time practising controlling your motorcycle while giving arm signals.

Practise

- with one hand and then with the other
- before you ride on the road.

Give arm signals in good time. Don't try to keep up the signal all the way through a turn. You'll need both hands on the handlebars to make any turn safely.

I intend to move out to the right or turn right

I intend to move in to the left or turn left

I intend to slow down or to stop

Signals to traffic controllers

I want to turn right

I want to turn left

I want to go straight on

Arm signals at speed When travelling at speed on the open road, arm signals can upset your stability. At speed it's safer to rely on your direction indicators, if fitted.

Arm signals at pedestrian crossings When slowing down or stopping at a pedestrian crossing consider using an arm signal. This tells

- following traffic
- approaching traffic
- waiting pedestrians

that you're slowing down.

Remember, approaching traffic and pedestrians can't see your brake lights.

Arm signals aren't a substitute for faulty direction indicators. The law requires that if direction indicators are fitted they must work.

Direction indicator signals

Indicator lamps are close together on a motorcycle and can be difficult to see. On some smaller machines the direction indicators don't show up very well in bright sunlight.

- Consider giving an arm signal if you think your direction indicators are difficult to see.
- Position yourself correctly and in good time for the manoeuvre you intend to perform.

I intend to move in to the left or turn left or stop on the left

I intend to move out to the right or turn right

I am slowing down or stopping

Other types of signals

Stop lamps Stop lamps come on when you apply the brakes. On a modern motorcycle the stop lamps are activated by the rear brake pedal. On many machines the front brake lever will also activate the stop lamps.

The stop lamps warn following traffic that you're braking. Help other road users by

- braking in good time
- slowing down gradually
- signalling in good time. Give an arm signal if necessary.

Flashing headlamps You should only flash your headlamp as an alternative to the horn to warn others that you're there. Assume that other drivers mean the same.

Don't flash at anyone to go ahead or turn.

If someone flashes their headlamps at you make sure that

- you understand what they mean
- it's you they're signalling to.

Never assume it's a signal to proceed.

Horn Sound the horn only if

- you think someone may not have seen you
- to warn other road users of your presence, for example at blind bends or junctions.

Sounding the horn doesn't give you the right of way. Always be prepared to stop.

You must not sound your horn

- between 11.30 pm and 7 am in a built-up area
- when your motorcycle is stationary, unless a moving vehicle poses a danger.

Never use your horn as a rebuke or to attract attention.

On high-speed roads drivers may not be able to hear your horn. In daylight, riding with your dipped headlamp on can help you to be seen.

Whether using indicators, arm signals, headlamps or horn, always think about your signal.

- is it necessary?
- is it helpful?
- is it misleading?

When you do signal, do so

- in good time
- clearly
- correctly.

Leave other road users in no doubt about your intentions. Giving signals properly is an important part of safe motorcycling.

Timing of signals

Whether you're giving arm signals or using direction indicators

- give your signal early enough to allow other road users to see and act on it
- don't give a signal so early that its meaning could mislead.

The illustration shows how a signal given too early could mislead. The driver of the red car might pull out, thinking the motorcyclist is turning.

Conflicting signals

A signal must have one clear meaning. For example, signalling right to pass a parked vehicle might mislead. Other traffic may think that you intend to turn right or to pull over on the right. Avoid giving signals which could have two meanings.

Cancelling signals   Very few motorcycles have self-cancelling indicators. It's very important that you cancel a signal when you've completed the manoeuvre. Failure to cancel a signal could mislead another road user and cause an accident.

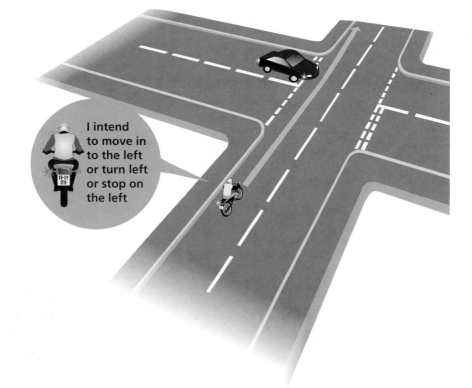

I intend to move in to the left or turn left or stop on the left

Moving off at an angle

When moving off at an angle – for instance, around a parked car – use the same procedure as for 'Moving off' covered earlier in this chapter.

Just before you move off ask yourself

- at what angle should I move out?
- how far will this take me into the road?

Your decision will depend on

- how close you are to the vehicle or object in front
- how wide the vehicle is ahead
- oncoming traffic.

Check all round for other vehicles and signal if necessary.

- Give yourself time to steer around the vehicle or object.
- Tight clutch and steering control are needed as you move off. Release the clutch completely as you clear the obstruction.
- Allow room for someone to open a door, if you're moving off around a vehicle.
- Be ready to brake – a pedestrian might step out from the other side of the vehicle or object.

Moving off uphill

Use the same procedure as for moving off straight ahead covered under 'Moving off' earlier in this chapter. Be aware that

- your motorcycle will tend to roll back. To avoid this, you must use the throttle, clutch and brakes together
- you may need to use more throttle when moving off uphill than you would when moving off on the level.

Remember

Allow a safe gap in any traffic because your motorcycle may be slower pulling away and building up speed.

The motorcycle will stall if

- you hold the rear brake on too long
- you release the clutch too quickly
- you don't use enough throttle.

When you've mastered the technique then practise moving off uphill without rolling backwards, from behind a parked vehicle.

Stopping the engine

This safe sequence applies to most motorcycles:

- close the throttle fully
- make sure that the gear selector is in neutral
- switch the ignition key to 'off'. Take out the key in the 'lock' position if you're leaving your machine
- turn the fuel tap to 'off' (if fitted).

Signs are an essential part of any traffic system.

They tell you about the rules you must obey and warn you about the hazards you can meet on the road ahead.

Signs can be in the form of words or symbols on panels, road markings, beacons, bollards or traffic lights.

This section deals with the various types of traffic signs and their meaning.

The topics covered

- the purpose of traffic signs
- signs giving warning
- signs giving orders
- signs giving directions and other information
- road markings
- traffic lights
- traffic calming
- level crossings.

The purpose of traffic signs

To do its job, a sign must give its message clearly and early enough for you to

*   see it
*   understand it
*   act safely on it.

Symbols

Symbols are used as much as possible because they're

*   more easily recognised and understood
*   mainly standard, particularly throughout Europe.

Recognising signs – the basic rules

You'll recognise traffic signs more easily if you understand some basic rules. The shape and colour of the main groups are

*   circular signs, which give orders
*   triangular signs, which warn
*   rectangular signs, which inform and give directions
*   road markings, which can do any of these three things
*   traffic lights.

Signs giving warning

Usually a red triangle pointing upwards, with a symbol or words on a white background.

These warn you of a hazard you might not otherwise be able to recognise in time, for example a bend, hill or hump backed bridge.

The sign will make clear what the hazard is. You must decide what to do about it.

Examples of warning signs

Narrowing roads

These tell you which side the road is narrowing from (sometimes both sides), and should warn you against overtaking until you have had a chance to assess the hazard.

Children and schools

The warning here is: watch out for children dashing out into the road, especially during school arrival and leaving times. Look out for school crossing patrols.

Low bridge sign

An oncoming vehicle might have to use the centre of the road to make use of any extra headroom there.

Junctions

These tell you what type of junction is ahead: T-junction, crossroads, roundabout, staggered junction and so on. The priority through the junction is indicated by the broader line.

Sharp change of direction chevrons

These may be used

• where the road changes direction sharply enough to create a hazard

• to reinforce a bend warning sign where stronger emphasis is needed.

Other hazards

If there's no special sign for a particular hazard, a general hazard warning sign is used: a red triangle with an exclamation mark on a white background.

It will have a plate underneath telling you what the hazard is, e.g., fallen tree.

Signs giving orders

Signs which give orders can be

- mandatory signs; these tell you what you **must** do
- prohibitory signs; these tell you what you **must not** do.

Mandatory signs

Mostly circular signs with white symbols and borders on a blue background.

For example

- mini roundabout
- keep left
- turn left.

In addition

- 'Stop – children' sign (lollipop) carried by school crossing patrol. This is circular with black lettering on a yellow background
- 'Stop' in white on a red background, often manually controlled at roadworks
- 'Stop' and 'Give way' signs appear at junctions and are very important for everyone's guidance and safety.

'Stop' signs

These are octagonal, with white lettering on a red background.

Usually at a junction with a limited zone of vision. Always accompanied by a stop line marked on the road. The line tells you how far forward you should go before stopping at the position from which you look, assess and decide if it is safe to proceed (Position, Speed, Look). See Part nine, 'The junction routine'.

What you must do at 'Stop' signs

- Stop (even if you can see the road is clear).
- Wait until you can enter the major road without causing other drivers to change speed or direction.

'Give way' signs

These consist of

- a red triangle pointing downwards
- black lettering on a white background.

They are always accompanied by road markings. However some junctions only have the 'Give way' lines. This is usually where there's relatively little traffic.

'Give way' signs and/or road markings show you that traffic on the road you want to enter has priority.

The double broken lines across the road show you where to stop, if necessary, to take your final look.

What you must do at 'give way' signs

- give way to traffic already on the major road
- delay entering the major road until you can do so without causing any traffic already on the major road to change speed or direction.

Remember

- Look
- Assess
- Decide
- Act.

Prohibitory signs

These tell you what you **must not** do.

They are easy to recognise by their circular shape and red border. The message is given by symbols, words or figures, or a combination of these.

Exceptions

- 'No entry' sign: circular with white border and red background
- 'Bus lane' sign.

Speed limit signs

A red circle with a number on a white background shows the speed limit.

A white disc with a black diagonal line cancels the previous speed limit, but you must not exceed the national speed limit for the type of road you're on.

Repeater signs are a small form of the original speed limit sign which are fitted to lamp-posts to remind you of the speed limit.

Where there are lamp-posts, you should assume that the 30 mph speed limit normally applies, unless there are repeater signs showing a different speed limit.

Signs giving directions and other information

These help you find and follow the road you want. They can also direct you to the nearest railway station, car park, or other facility or attraction.

The colours of these signs vary with the type of road.

For example:

*   motorways – blue with white letters and border
*   primary routes, except motorways – green with white letters and border, route numbers shown in yellow
*   other routes – white with black letters and black or blue border.

All these roads may also display tourist signs, which are brown with white letters and border.

Types of signs giving directions on primary routes

Advance direction signs   You will see these before you reach the junction. They enable you to decide which direction to take and to prepare yourself.

Direction signs at the junction   These show you the way to take as you reach the junction.

Route confirmatory signs   Positioned after the junction, these confirm which road you're on.

These signs also tell you distances and places on your route. If the route number is in brackets, it means that the road leads to that route.

Information signs

These tell you

*   where to find parking places, telephones, camping sites, etc.
*   about no-through roads, etc.

Road markings

Markings on the road give information, orders or warnings. They can be used with signs on posts or on their own.

Their advantages are

- they can often be seen when other signs are hidden by traffic
- they can give a continuing message as you travel along the road.

As a general rule, the more paint, the more important the message.

Lines across the road

'Give way' lines

Double broken white lines across your half of the road show that traffic on the road you want to enter has priority. The lines show where you should stop, if necessary, to take your final look. These may also be found on a roundabout where traffic **on** the roundabout is required to give way to those joining.

A single broken line is normally found at the entrance to a roundabout. This tells you that traffic coming from your immediate right has priority and you must give way.

Single 'Stop' lines

A single continuous line across your half of the road shows where you must stop

- at junctions with 'Stop' signs
- at junctions controlled by police or traffic lights
- at level crossings
- at swing bridges or ferries.

Lines along the road

Double white lines

The most important of these are double white lines and they have rules for

- overtaking
- parking.

Overtaking When the line nearest you is continuous, you must not cross or straddle it except when it is safe and you want to

- enter or leave a side road or entrance on the opposite side of the road
- pass a stationary vehicle
- pass a road maintenance vehicle, pedal cycle or horse moving at 10 mph or less.

If there's a broken white line on your side and a continuous white line on the other, you may cross both lines to overtake. Make sure you can complete the manoeuvre before reaching a solid line on your side.

Arrows on the road often warn that there's a double white line coming up. Don't begin to overtake when you see them.

Parking On a road marked with double white lines you must not stop or park, even if one of the lines is broken. You may, however, stop for a moment to pick up or drop off passengers.

Hatch markings There are dangerous areas where it is necessary to separate the streams of traffic completely, such as a sharp bend or hump, or where traffic turning right needs protection. These areas are painted with white chevrons or diagonal stripes. Remember:

- where the boundary line is solid, do not enter except in an emergency
- where the boundary line is broken, you should not ride on the markings unless you can see that it is safe to do so.

Single broken lines

Watch out for places where the single broken line down the centre of the road gets longer. This shows a hazard ahead.

Lane dividers

Short broken white lines are used on wide carriageways to divide them into lanes. You should keep between them unless you are overtaking or turning right.

Lanes for specific types of vehicle

Bus and cycle lanes are shown by signs and road markings. In some one-way streets these vehicles are permitted to travel against the normal flow of traffic. These are known as contraflow lanes.

Bus lanes Only vehicles shown on the sign may use the lane during the times of operation which are also shown on the sign. Outside those periods all vehicles can use the bus lane.

Where there are no times shown, the bus lane is in operation for 24 hours a day.

Don't use bus lanes when they are in operation unless motorcycles are shown on the sign as permitted vehicles.

Cycle lanes Don't ride or park in a cycle lane marked by a solid white line during the times of operation shown on the signs.

If the cycle lane is marked by a broken line, don't ride or park in it unless it is unavoidable.

Remember

If you park in a cycle lane at any time you can make it very dangerous for any cyclist who is using that lane.

Reflective studs

These are

- red on the left-hand side of the road
- white on the lane or centre-of-road lines
- amber on the right-hand edge of the carriageway on dual carriageways and motorways
- green between the carriageway and lay-bys, side roads and slip roads.

At road works, fluorescent green/yellow studs may be used to help identify the lanes in operation.

Box junction markings

Yellow crisscross lines mark a box junction.

Their purpose is to keep the junction clear by preventing traffic from stopping in the path of crossing traffic.

You must not enter a box junction unless your exit road is clear. But you can enter the box when you want to turn right and you're only prevented from doing so by oncoming traffic.

If there's a vehicle already on the junction waiting to turn right, you're free to enter behind it and wait to turn right – providing that you won't block any oncoming traffic wanting to turn right.

If there are a number of vehicles waiting to turn, it's unlikely you'll be able to proceed before the traffic signals change.

Words on the road

Words on the road surface usually have a clear meaning such as 'Stop', 'Slow', 'Keep clear'.

When they show a part of the road is reserved for certain vehicles, for example, buses, taxis or ambulances, don't ride there.

Destination markings

Near a busy junction, lanes sometimes have destination markings or road numbers on the road surface.

These enable you to get into the correct lane early, even if advance direction road signs are obscured.

Schools

Yellow zigzags are often marked on the road outside schools, along with the words 'School – keep clear'. Do not stop or park there. The markings are to make sure that

• drivers passing and
• children crossing

have a clear, unrestricted view of the crossing area.

Lane arrows

These tell you which lane to take for the direction you want.

Where the road is wide enough, you may find one arrow pointing in each direction:

- left in the left-hand lane
- straight ahead in the centre lane
- right in the right-hand lane.

Some arrows might be combined, depending on how busy the junction is. If the road is only wide enough for two lanes, arrows might have two directions combined

- straight ahead and left in the left-hand lane
- straight ahead and right in the right-hand lane.

Left- and right-turn arrows are placed well before a junction to help you get into the correct lane in good time. They don't indicate the exact point at which you should turn. It's especially important to remember this at right turns.

Speed reduction lines

Raised yellow lines may be painted across the carriageway at the approach to

- roundabouts
- reduced speed limits when entering a village
- particular hazards.

The purpose of these lines is to make you aware of your speed after a period of travel at higher speeds. Reduce your speed in good time.

Traffic lights

Traffic lights have three lights which change in a set cycle

- red
- red and amber
- green
- amber
- red.

What the colours mean

- red – stop and wait at the stop line
- red and amber – stop and wait. Don't go until green shows
- green – go if the way is clear
- amber – stop, unless
  - you've already crossed the line
  - you're so close to it that pulling up might cause an accident.

Approaching green traffic lights

Approach traffic lights as you would any other junction. Keep your speed down.

Don't speed up to 'beat the lights'. Be ready to stop, especially if the lights have been green for some time.

Green filter arrow

A green arrow in a traffic light means you can filter in the direction the arrow is pointing, even if the main light is not showing green.

Don't enter this lane unless you want to go in the direction shown by the arrow.

When turning left or right at traffic lights take special care, and give way to pedestrians already crossing.

OSM/PSL routine

Use the OSM and PSL routines as you approach the lights (Observation–Signal –Manoeuvre, Position–Speed–Look). See Part Nine, 'The junction routine'.

Pay attention to lane markings and get into the correct lane in good time. Be prepared to stop.

Advance stop lines

At some traffic lights there are advance stop lines to allow cyclists to position themselves ahead of other traffic.

Stop at the first white line. Do not encroach on the marked area, which is reserved for cyclists only. Allow the cyclists time and space to move off when the lights change to green.

In some areas there are bus advance areas, these should be treated in the same way as those provided for cyclists.

Special traffic lights

These are often used to control traffic where low-flying aircraft pass over the road, or at swing or lifting bridges, or other special sites such as fire stations.

They may either be

*   normal traffic lights (red, amber and green) – follow the normal rules
*   double red flashing lights – stop when the red lights are flashing.

If traffic lights fail

If the traffic lights fail, proceed with caution. Treat the situation as you would an **unmarked** junction.

School crossing warning

Two amber lights flashing alternately warn traffic of a school crossing point ahead at some busy locations.

Keep your speed down and proceed with great care.

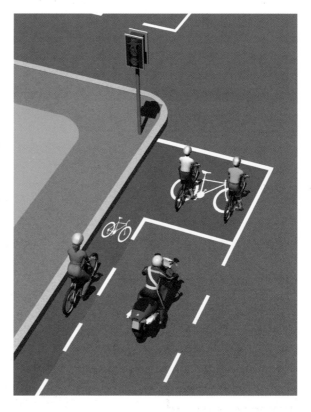

Traffic calming

Traffic calming measures are used to encourage people to reduce speed more than they might otherwise do. They are used in particularly sensitive areas where it is considered that a reduction in speed would benefit the immediate community.

Various features can be provided to slow down the speed of traffic

- road humps
- road narrowings, central islands and chicanes
- mini roundabouts

20 mph zones

Some traffic-calmed areas are indicated only by a 20 mph speed limit sign.

This speed limit sign, in addition to advising the maximum speed limit, also indicates that there may be traffic calming features within the signed zone and these may not be individually signed.

You should ride at a steady speed within the speed limit, and avoid frequent acceleration and deceleration within these areas.

Road humps

These may be round or flat topped humps laid across the carriageway. They may be used on roads where there is a speed limit of 30 mph or less.

In some areas the humps are in the form of 'cushions' which only cover part of the lane and are designed so that larger vehicles, especially buses, can straddle them.

If these are provided outside 20 mph zones, there will normally be

- warning signs at the beginning of the section of road where the hump or series of humps are installed
- triangle and edge line markings at each hump.

Road narrowings

Roads may be narrowed by the use of 'build outs' on one or both sides of the road.

If these are provided outside 20 mph zones, there will normally be

- warning signs indicating which side of the road narrowing occurs
- 'Give way' road markings on one side of the road accompanied by signs advising priority for oncoming vehicles.

If these are on your side of the road, you must always give way to vehicles approaching from the other direction.

If priority is not given in either direction, then ensure you can pass through the narrowing without endangering vehicles approaching from the other direction. You should not accelerate as you approach the narrowing, but be prepared to slow down or give way to approaching traffic. Don't try to squeeze through at the same time as these vehicles.

Mini roundabouts

Mini roundabouts are often used as part of traffic-calming schemes to break up a long road into shorter sections and allow traffic to join from minor roads.

Methods of dealing with mini roundabouts are given in Part nine, under 'Roundabouts'.

Give way to oncoming vehicles

Priority over oncoming vehicles

Drivers of
LARGE or SLOW
VEHICLES
must phone
and get permission
to cross

LARGE means
over 55' long or 9'6" wide
or 38 tonnes total weight
SLOW means 5mph or less

DRIVERS OF LONG
LOW VEHICLES
phone
before crossing

KEEP
CROSSING
CLEAR

ANOTHER TRAIN
COMING
if lights
continue to show

KEEP
CROSSING
CLEAR

Level crossings

At a level crossing, the road crosses railway lines. Approach and cross with care.

Never

- ride onto the crossing unless the road is clear on the other side
- stop on or just after the crossing
- park close to the crossing.

Most crossings have full or half barriers.

Open crossings have no gates or barriers.

Either type may be controlled by a steady amber light followed by twin flashing red lights which warn of an approaching train. An audible alarm to warn pedestrians will also sound once the lights show. You must obey the lights' signals.

Don't

- move onto the crossing after the lights show
- stop on the crossing if the amber light or audible alarm starts to operate – **keep going** if you're already on the crossing
- zigzag round half barriers.

If the train goes by and the red lights continue to flash, or the audible alarm changes tone, you must wait because another train is approaching.

Crossings without signals

At crossings with no lights, **stop** when the gates or barriers begin to close.

User-operated crossings with signals

Some crossings with gates or barriers have 'Stop' signs and small red and green lights. Do not cross when the red light is on because a train is approaching. Cross only when the green is on.

Open the gates or barriers on **both** sides of the crossing. Check the green light is still on and cross promptly. Close the gates or barriers when you're clear of the crossing.

User-operated crossings without signals

Some crossings have gates but no attendant or signals. At these crossings

- stop
- look both ways
- listen and make sure that no train is approaching.

If there's a railway telephone contact the signal operator to make sure it's safe to cross.

Open the gates on both sides of the crossing and check again that no train is coming before crossing promptly.

Once you've cleared the crossing

- close both gates
- inform the signal operator, if there's a telephone.

Always give way to trains – they can't stop easily.

With lights

Without lights

Open crossings

At an open crossing with no gates, barriers, attendant or traffic signals, there will be a 'Give way' sign.

Look both ways, listen and make sure there's no train coming before you cross.

Breakdowns

If your motorcycle breaks down on the crossing

• get yourself, any passenger and your motorcycle clear of the crossing immediately.

If you can't move your motorcycle immediately

• get yourself and any passenger clear of the crossing

• if there's a railway telephone, use it **immediately** to inform the signal operator: **follow any instructions you're given**

• **if there's time** before a train arrives, move your motorcycle clear of the crossing

• if the alarm sounds, or the amber light comes on, **get clear of the crossing at once – the train will not be able to stop.**

Tram crossings (LRTs)

Look for traffic signs which show where trams cross the road.

Treat them the same as normal railway crossings.

Remember

These modern trams are very silent. Take extra care and look both ways before crossing.

PART EIGHT ON THE ROAD

The previous parts have shown you how to use the controls and ride your motorcycle. Road signs and markings have been explained and now you need to know the skills that will let you cope effectively with various road situations.

The topics covered

- awareness and anticipation
- mirrors
- rear observation
- road position
- stopping distance
- the road surface
- skidding
- separation distance
- overtaking
- obstructions
- pedestrian crossings
- tunnels
- parking
- security.

Awareness and anticipation

In any traffic situation there are some things that are obviously going to happen, as well as some things that **might** happen.

To anticipate is to take action when you expect something will or might happen.

You can anticipate what might happen by making early use of the available information on the road.

Ask yourself:

- what am I likely to find?
- what are other road users trying to do?
- should I speed up or slow down?
- do I need to stop?

Changing conditions

Traffic conditions change constantly and you need to

- check and re-check what's going on around you
- be alert all the time to changes in conditions, and think ahead.

The degree to which you need to anticipate varies according to those conditions.

Difficult conditions

You'll find it more difficult to decide what might happen when

- the light or the weather is poor
- the traffic is heavy
- the route is unfamiliar.

Types of road

Similarly, types of road will affect how much you can anticipate.

It's easier in light traffic to anticipate what other drivers might do. It is more difficult on a busy single carriageway, dual carriageway or motorway, where their options are greater.

Riding ahead

Read the road ahead to anticipate what might happen.

You need to be alert and observant at all times.

Assess the movement of all other road users, including pedestrians, on the whole stretch of road you're travelling on.

Take in as much as possible of the road

- ahead
- behind
- to each side.

You should keep scanning the area in your view and

- be able to observe the middle distance and far distance as well as the area immediately in front
- glance frequently in the mirror to see what's happening in the area you've just passed.

Observation

If you're a new rider, you'll tend to give more of your attention to controlling the motorcycle.

Practise reading the road. You don't have to be riding to do this. You can do it as a passenger on a motorcycle or in a car or bus.

Look out for

- other vehicles and pedestrians
- signals given by others
- road signs and markings
- the type and condition of the road surface
- movements of vehicles well ahead of you, as well as the one immediately in front
- side roads or hills ahead. The building line may show these
- buses signalling to move out from bus stops.

Clues

Look out for clues to help you to act safely and sensibly on what you see.

Watch smaller details in built-up areas where traffic conditions change rapidly. Observe other road users' actions and reactions.

Reflections in shop windows can often give important information where vision is restricted.

A pedestrian approaching a zebra crossing might step out into the road sooner than you think.

Take care approaching parked vehicles, especially if someone is in the driving seat.

Watch out for a driver stopping to set down or pick up a passenger. You may find they move off without warning or without checking in the mirrors or looking around.

When following a bus, watch for passengers standing up inside: the bus will probably stop shortly.

Remember

Try to anticipate the actions of other road users.

Be aware

Observing is not just seeing How much you can see depends on how well you can see.

Your eyesight can change without you being aware of it. Have regular eyesight checks.

Your ears can also warn of what's happening around you.

At works entrances and schools you should expect an increase in pedestrians, cyclists and vehicles. Watch for vehicles picking up and setting down at school times – buses as well as cars.

Emergency vehicles

Look and listen for emergency vehicles such as fire engines, ambulances, police and other emergency services using blue, red or green flashing lights or sirens.

You should try to keep out of their way. Check where they are coming from: behind (mirrors), ahead or, more importantly, across your path.

Do not panic. Watch for the path of the emergency vehicle and take any action you can to try to help it get through. If necessary pull into the side of the road and stop, but do not endanger yourself or other road users.

Riding in busy areas

When riding in busy areas, you should be especially alert to all the possible hazards already mentioned.

You should also be particularly aware of your speed and always ride at a speed appropriate to the conditions.

The speed limit is the absolute maximum and does not always mean that it is safe for you to ride at that speed. For example, in a narrow residential street with cars parked on either side, you may need to reduce your speed considerably.

Mirrors

Mirrors must be adjusted to give a clear view behind. They should be kept clean and smear-free.

When you're riding you might find that your elbows or shoulders obstruct the view behind. To overcome this, adjust your mirrors to the best position. If this problem remains you can solve it by extending the mirrors with longer stems.

If your mirrors vibrate your view will be distorted. Your motorcycle dealer may be able to offer advice on how to reduce the vibration.

Using the mirrors

Glancing regularly into your mirrors will keep you up to date with the traffic situation behind. Use your mirrors before

- signalling
- changing direction
- overtaking
- changing lanes
- slowing down or stopping.

Use your mirrors together with looking behind, where necessary.

Just looking isn't enough!

Whether you look in your mirrors or over your shoulder

- you must act on what you see
- think about how your actions will affect following traffic.

Rear observation

Rear observation refers to a combination of mirror checks and looking behind which ensures you're always fully aware of what's happening behind you.

Before you signal or change direction or speed you must know how your actions will affect following traffic. You also have to know when traffic is likely to overtake or come alongside you.

Looking behind is important because not all motorcycles are fitted with mirrors, and mirrors don't always give a clear view behind, leaving significant blind spots. There will be times when you need to look round to see the full picture.

Looking behind also warns other drivers that you may be about to signal or alter course.

When should you look behind?

Use judgement in deciding when to look behind. Obviously when you're looking behind you're not looking ahead. This could be hazardous if, for example, you're close to the vehicle in front or if you're overtaking at speed. Equally there are situations when it is dangerous not to look behind, such as at a right turn into a minor road.

Take rear observation when you're about to change position or speed as you approach and negotiate a hazard. This might be before

- moving off
- turning left or right
- overtaking
- changing lanes
- slowing or stopping.

Warning Looking over your shoulder too often or at the wrong moment can be hazardous. In the time you take to look behind, you

- lose touch with what's going on in front
- run the risk of veering off course.

At high speed or in congested moving traffic your attention needs to be focused ahead. In these situations time your rearward checks carefully. Combine

- regular and sensible use of the mirrors
- the 'lifesaver' check into the blind area before altering course (see below).

The 'lifesaver' check

The 'lifesaver' is a last check over the shoulder into the blind spot to make sure nothing unexpected is happening before committing yourself to a manoeuvre. If you're turning, use it to check the blind spot on the side you intend to turn. Use your judgement about when to use it: in congested urban situations a lifesaver check is normally essential, especially when turning right into a minor road, but during high speed overtaking, when you're certain what's happening behind, it's often safer to keep your eyes on what's happening ahead.

The blind area

The blind area is the area behind and to either side of you which isn't covered by mirrors. It's very important to check for traffic in this area before

- moving off
- changing direction
- changing lane.

Road position

As a general rule, keep to the centre of the lane. On a single carriageway (two-way traffic) that is halfway between the centre of the road and the left side.

Your position will depend on

- the width of the road
- the road surface
- your view ahead
- any obstructions.

Your position should allow you to

- be easily seen by traffic ahead, particularly vehicles emerging from junctions
- be seen in the mirror of any vehicle in front
- move over to the left to create more room for oncoming traffic that's passing stationary vehicles or other obstructions.

Keep clear of the gutter, where there are often potholes and loose grit.

Keep clear of the centre of the road. You might

- obstruct overtaking traffic
- put yourself in danger from oncoming traffic
- encourage following traffic to overtake you on your left.

The correct position   You should always be in the correct position for the route you're going to take.

- Keep to the left if you're going straight ahead or turning left.
- Keep as close to the centre of the road as is safe when you're turning right.

Your position is important not only for safety, but also to allow the free flow of traffic. A badly positioned vehicle can hold up traffic in either direction.

One-way streets   Position according to whether you intend to go ahead, turn left, or turn right.

- To turn left, keep to the left-hand lane.
- To turn right, keep to the right-hand lane, provided there are no obstructions or parked vehicles on the right-hand side of the road you are in.
- To go ahead, be guided by the road markings. If there is no specific lane for ahead, select the most appropriate lane, normally the left, in good time.

Follow the road markings and get into the correct lane as soon as possible and stay in this lane. Watch for drivers who may change lane suddenly.

Traffic in one-way streets often flows freely. Watch out for vehicles coming past on either side of you.

Lane discipline

You should always follow lane markings, which are there for two reasons:

- they make the best possible use of road space
- they guide the traffic.

Keeping to the lane markings is vital.

Position yourself in good time If you find you're in the wrong lane, don't try to change by cutting across the path of others at the last moment. Carry on in your lane and find another way back to your route.

Changing lanes Position your vehicle according to your route. Always check behind and signal in good time before you change lanes, and

- never weave from lane to lane
- never change lanes at the last minute
- always stay in the middle of your lane until you need to change.

In heavy and slow moving traffic Don't

- change lanes suddenly
- keep changing lanes
- weave in and out
- obstruct 'Keep clear' markings. Watch out for these in congested, slow moving traffic, especially at exits for emergency vehicles.

Allow for

- pedestrians crossing
- cyclists moving up the nearside
- large vehicles needing to straddle lanes before turning
- doors opening.

Riding ahead Keep to the left-hand lane wherever possible.

Don't use the right-hand lane just because you're travelling at speed.

On a carriageway with four or more lanes, don't use the lanes on the right unless signs or markings allow you to do so. Peak hour 'tidal flow' systems might permit or forbid use of these lanes, depending on the time of day.

Bus and cycle lanes These are separate lanes shown by signs and road markings. Do not enter these lanes unless permitted by the signs.

Approaching a road junction

Look well ahead for signs and markings.

If you have two lanes in your direction and

*   you intend to turn left, stay in the left-hand lane
*   you intend to go ahead, stay in the left-hand lane unless otherwise indicated
*   you intend to turn right, move to the right-hand lane in good time.

Don't try to gain an advantage by using an incorrect lane. Trying to change back to the proper lane at, or near, the junction is a risky business.

If you have three lanes in your direction and you intend to

*   turn left, stay in the left-hand lane
*   go ahead, take the left-hand lane (unless there are left filter signs) or the middle lane, or be guided by road markings
*   turn right, take the right-hand lane.

Slip road

Some junctions also have a slip road.

Get into the left-hand lane in good time before entering the slip road. You'll be able to slow down to turn left without holding up other traffic.

Stopping distance

It's important for you to know the stopping distance at all speeds. This is the distance your motorcycle travels

- from the moment you realise you must brake
- to the moment your machine stops.

Always ride so that you can stop safely within the distance you can see to be clear.

Stopping distance depends on

- how fast you're going
- whether you're travelling uphill, on the level or downhill
- the weather and the state of the road
- the condition of your brakes and tyres
- your ability, especially your reaction times.

Stopping distance divides into

- thinking distance
- braking distance.

Thinking distance

'Thinking distance' is from the point where you see the hazard to the point where you brake. This distance will vary from rider to rider and is dependent upon reaction time. Reaction times are affected by

- age
- physical and mental condition
- health
- time of day
- alcohol or drugs.

An alert and fit rider needs 0.75 of a second thinking time. That means that at 50 mph you'll travel about 15 metres (about 50 feet) **before you begin to brake.**

Typical Stopping Distances

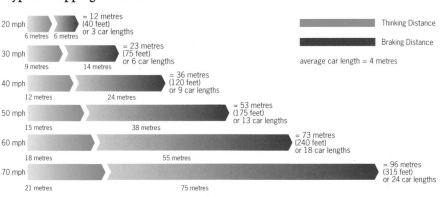

20 mph = 12 metres (40 feet) or 3 car lengths
6 metres 6 metres

30 mph = 23 metres (75 feet) or 6 car lengths
9 metres   14 metres

40 mph = 36 metres (120 feet) or 9 car lengths
12 metres   24 metres

50 mph = 53 metres (175 feet) or 13 car lengths
15 metres   38 metres

60 mph = 73 metres (240 feet) or 18 car lengths
18 metres   55 metres

70 mph = 96 metres (315 feet) or 24 car lengths
21 metres   75 metres

Thinking Distance

Braking Distance

average car length = 4 metres

Braking distance

'Braking distance' is from the point where you begin to brake to the point where you stop.

Braking distance depends upon

- road conditions
- tyre condition
- brake efficiency
- suspension efficiency
- load. It takes longer to stop if you're carrying a passenger
- rider ability.

Most of all, braking distance varies with speed. At 30 mph your braking distance will be about 14 metres (about 45 feet) while at 70 mph that distance will increase to about 75 metres (about 245 feet). That's just over double the speed but more than **five times** the braking distance.

Overall stopping distance

Your overall stopping distance also increases dramatically as you increase your road speed. The scale of the stopping distance as it changes with speed is illustrated.

23 metres (75 feet)

96 metres (315 feet)

The stopping distance at 70 mph is more than four times the stopping distance at 30 mph.

The road surface

The state of the road surface is very important to motorcyclists. Only a small part of the motorcycle tyre makes contact with the road. Any change in the surface can therefore affect the stability of your motorcycle.

Be on the lookout for poor road surfaces. Beware of

- loose surfaces, such as chippings, gravel, mud and leaves
- potholes and uneven surfaces
- inspection covers, especially when wet
- oil patches and spilt fuel, especially at roundabouts, bus stops and filling stations
- tar banding around road repairs
- painted road markings

- rails set into the road for trams or light rapid transit (LRT) systems. These can affect your steering and present a hazard when braking
- any shiny road surface. At junctions, frequent braking and acceleration can polish the surface.

If you can safely avoid riding on slippery surfaces then do so. If you have to ride on a slippery surface slow down well in advance. Don't swerve suddenly to avoid a poor surface.

If you find yourself on a slippery surface check the traffic, then gradually slow down.

Part twelve, 'Riding in bad weather', contains information on the effects of weather on the road surface.

Skidding

A skid is when tyres

- lose their grip on the road surface
- veer off the steered course
- reduce the effect of the brakes (by sliding over the road surface).

Causes of skidding

- heavy or uncoordinated braking, which locks one or both wheels
- excessive acceleration, causing the rear wheel to spin
- swerving (a sudden change of direction)
- leaning over too far when cornering, causing one or both tyres to lose grip.

A good rider tries to avoid skidding. The loss of control which can arise from a skid can be lethal.

Swerving (changing direction suddenly)

Leaning too far over when cornering

Dealing with skids

Skids can happen suddenly. You need to know how to regain control when skidding occurs.

Excessive acceleration   If you've caused a skid by excessive acceleration

- the rear wheelspin can cause your machine to slide sideways. Steer in the direction that your machine is sliding
- ease off the throttle to regain control.

Braking   If you've caused a skid by braking

- release the brakes to let the wheels start turning again
- reapply the brakes as firmly as the conditions will permit.

Your natural instincts when dealing with a skid caused by excessive braking will be to brake even harder. You must learn to overcome such instincts if you're to regain control.

Correcting a skid

- Steer into the skid. If the machine is sliding to the right, steer to the right. If the machine is sliding to the left, steer to the left.
- Keep your feet on the footrests. Putting your feet to the ground on a moving motorcycle could upset your balance.

Skids are a lot easier to get into than they are to get out of. Remember, skid control is an emergency measure – it's no substitute for skid avoidance.

Bike skidding to the left

Direction of steering to correct skid

- **Ease off brake**
- **Steer to left**

Separation distance

How far must you keep from the vehicle in front? Ideally you should be no closer than the stopping distance that corresponds to your speed. In some traffic situations that may not be possible. The gap must never be less than your thinking distance, and much more if the road is wet or slippery.

One method of judging separation distance is to allow 1 metre (just over 3 feet) for each mph of your speed. For example, at 45 mph leave a gap of 45 metres (about 150 feet).

A useful technique for judging 1 metre per mph is to use the 'two-second rule'.

The two-second rule

In good conditions an experienced rider needs to be at least two seconds behind the vehicle in front.

To measure this gap

- select a stationary object on the side of the road, for example a road sign
- as the vehicle in front passes the object say to yourself, 'Only a fool breaks the two-second rule'.

If you reach the object before you finish saying the sentence, you're too close.

In bad weather, at least double this gap between you and the vehicle in front.

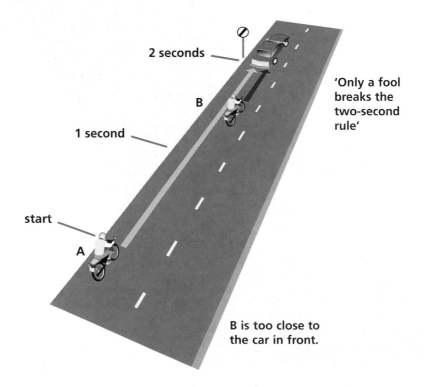

2 seconds

'Only a fool breaks the two-second rule'

B

1 second

start

A

B is too close to the car in front.

Separation distance behind

When the vehicle behind is following too
closely, slow down gradually. You need to
increase the gap between you and the vehicle
in front. This will give

*   you more time to brake if necessary
*   the following vehicle a better chance
    to overtake.

Overtaking

Don't overtake unless it's necessary. For example, don't rush to get past someone only to turn off shortly afterwards.

Ask yourself if it's really necessary. If you decide it is, you need to find a suitable place.

You must not overtake where to do so would cause you to break the law. Details are shown in *The Highway Code*.

In addition, some places are never suitable. For example, Don't overtake

- if your view ahead is blocked
- if others might not be able to see you
- if there isn't enough room
- if the road narrows
- if you're approaching a junction
- if you're within the zigzag area of a pedestrian crossing
- if there's a 'No overtaking' sign
- if you have to cross a continuous central white line on your side of the road. The exception to this rule is when it's safe to pass an obstruction such as a road maintenance vehicle, a cyclist or a horse. They must be either stationary or travelling at less than 10 mph
- if there's 'dead ground', that is, a dip in the road which might conceal an oncoming vehicle.

Judging speed and distance

If you're travelling at 50 mph and an oncoming vehicle is travelling at the same speed, you're approaching each other at 100 mph or 45 metres (about 150 feet) per second. This can be difficult to judge accurately so give yourself plenty of time.

Take great care if you're travelling on a two-way three-lane road. An oncoming vehicle might pull out to overtake while you're overtaking. Wearing bright clothing and riding with your dipped headlamp on will help oncoming drivers to see you. Nevertheless, be aware of the hazard.

When you're following slower traffic and looking for the chance to overtake, keep a safe distance. Staying back will help you to see past the vehicle in front, and give you time to react to its signals.

Filtering

The small size of a motorcycle makes it possible to filter through slow or stationary queues of traffic. Filtering requires great care and can expose you to additional hazards. You must comply with *The Highway Code* and when filtering you need to

- ride slowly and be prepared to stop
- watch for
  - vehicles suddenly changing lane
  - sudden opening of doors
  - pedestrians and cyclists
  - vehicles emerging or turning at junctions
  - road markings or studs which could upset your balance
- be ready to brake and/or use the horn if you don't think you've been seen.

Remember other road users may not be expecting a filtering motorcycle. Make yourself easy to see by wearing bright clothing and use your headlamp on dipped beam.

Before overtaking

Many danger spots are marked with double white lines along the road. Look out for arrows warning you to move over to the left as you are approaching these areas.

On three-lane roads, junction signs and hatch markings in the middle of the road are warnings not to overtake. Be ready to hold back in case traffic is waiting to turn right or slowing to turn left.

Watch the vehicle in front   Before overtaking, decide what the driver in front is likely to do by watching both them and the road ahead for a while. They might

- decide to overtake
- continue to drive at the speed of the vehicle ahead of them.
- intend to turn off soon
- have seen something ahead which you haven't.

Vehicles turning right   Research has shown that most overtaking accidents are caused by the overtaking vehicle hitting a vehicle which is turning right. To avoid this type of accident you should

- consciously check the indicators of the vehicle you are about to overtake
- assume that a vehicle that is slowing down is about to turn.

Following through   Never automatically follow an overtaking vehicle without being able to see for yourself that the way is clear. The vehicle in front

- obscures your view
- hides you from the view of oncoming traffic.

Always make your own decisions about overtaking based on

- what **you** see
- what **you** know.

Be patient. If in doubt, hold back.

There might not be enough time for both of you to overtake at once.

Overtaking procedure

To overtake, use the OSM/PSL routine:

O – Take **observation**, both well ahead and behind.

S – Consider **signalling.**

M – **Manoeuvre**; use PSL (below).

P – Check your **position**. Be near enough to the vehicle ahead to overtake smoothly when you're ready, but not so close that you can't get a good view of the road ahead.

S – Have you enough **speed** and acceleration to overtake? Be fast enough to keep up with the vehicle in front and with enough reserve power to pass it briskly.

You might need to change down to get extra acceleration when you're ready to start overtaking.

L – **Look**. Assess the whole situation:

- the state of the road
- what the driver ahead is doing or might be about to do
- any hazards
- the speed and position of oncoming vehicles
- the speed difference between you and oncoming vehicles.

If you have any doubts, don't overtake.

If you're satisfied that it's safe to overtake, apply OSM again.

When you overtake you should

- consider a 'lifesaver' glance just before you move out
- overtake as quickly as you can and don't cut in front of the vehicle you've just passed

- cancel your signal when you've finished overtaking
- never automatically follow an overtaking vehicle. Your view of the road ahead may be obstructed. If you can't see clearly ahead, wait.

Remember

When overtaking cyclists or horseriders give them plenty of room.

Never attempt to overtake just before turning left.

Overtaking on the left

You should never overtake on the left unless

- the vehicle in front is signalling an intention to turn right, and you can safely overtake on the left
- traffic is moving slowly in queues, and vehicles in the lane on your right are moving more slowly than you are.

Take care if there is a road to the left. Oncoming traffic turning right into it may be hidden by the vehicle you're overtaking.

Passing on the left

In addition you can go past on the inside of slower traffic when

- you're in a one-way street (but not a dual carriageway) where vehicles are allowed to pass on either side
- you're in the correct lane to turn left at a junction.

When overtaking, you must judge the speed of oncoming traffic. If in doubt, don't overtake.

Overtaking on dual carriageways

Don't overtake unless you're sure that you can do so safely. Use the appropriate parts of the OSM/PSL routine:

O – Use your mirrors. Take rear **observation** if necessary.

P – **Position** yourself so that you can see well ahead past the vehicle in front.

S – Make sure that you have enough reserve **speed** to overtake.

L – **Look** ahead to make sure that the lane you want to join is clear.

If you're satisfied that it's safe to overtake, use OSM again.

M – **Manoeuvre**. Don't forget the 'lifesaver' glance into the blind area before you change course. Overtake quickly and decisively. Cancel your signal promptly and return to the left lane only when you're clear of the vehicle you've overtaken. Don't cut in.

High-speed riding If you're travelling at high speed it's safer to combine regular, sensible use of the mirrors with the 'lifesaver' glance before changing course.

Lane discipline Use the left-hand lane unless the amount of slow-moving traffic would cause you to be constantly changing lanes. Don't weave from lane to lane.

Where there are three lanes, don't ride in the middle lane if the left lane is clear. Always return to the left lane when you've finished overtaking.

Obstructions

The secret of dealing with any obstruction lies in looking and planning well ahead, combined with early and sensible use of the OSM/PSL routine.

The decision to wait or go on will depend on

- the type and width of road
- whether the obstruction is on
  - your side of the road
  - the other side of the road
  - both sides of the road
- whether there is approaching traffic
- the room available.

As a general rule, if the obstruction is on your side of the road, approaching traffic will have priority.

Don't assume that you have priority if the obstruction is on the other side of the road. Always be prepared to give way.

Procedure

Look well ahead to identify the obstruction in good time before using the OSM/PSL routine.

O – Use your mirrors. Take rear **observation** if necessary.

S – **Signal** if necessary.

P – Decide on your **position**. Avoid keeping too far in to the left so that you have to change direction at the last minute; a gradual change of course is required. If you have to stop and wait, keep well back from the obstruction in a position that not only keeps your zone of vision open, but also doesn't impede the approaching traffic.

S – Adjust your **speed** as necessary. This will depend on the situation, but aim to regulate your speed to take a smooth and steady course without stopping.

L – Finally, **look** and assess the situation before you decide whether it's

- necessary to wait
- safe to proceed.

Obstructions on hills

These need special care. Give yourself an extra safety margin and brake earlier than normal, when necessary.

If you're travelling downhill and the obstruction is on the other side of the road, don't take your priority for granted. If it's safe, be prepared to let other traffic coming uphill, especially heavy vehicles, have a clear run. Your consideration will be appreciated.

Defensive riding

Don't follow through behind the vehicle in front without being able to see for yourself that the way is clear ahead.

Keep a safe distance from the obstruction and the approaching traffic. Where space is limited, reduce speed and take extra care. The smaller the gap, the lower the speed needs to be.

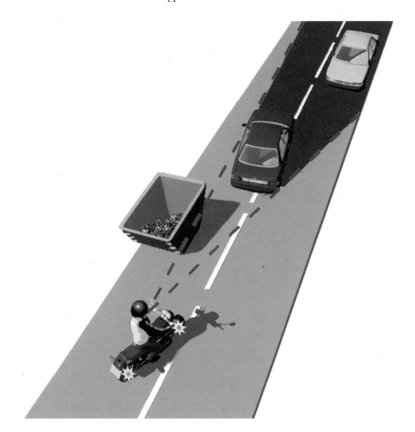

Pedestrian crossings

People on foot have certain rights of way at pedestrian crossings, but are safe only if everyone sticks to the rules and does the right thing.

Types of crossing

There are various types of pedestrian crossings

Zebra crossings are identified by flashing yellow beacons on both sides of the road and black and white stripes on the crossing. They also have white zigzag markings on both sides of the crossing and a give way line about a yard from the crossing, which marks the place for drivers to stop when necessary.

Zebra crossing

Pelican crossings are light-controlled crossings where the pedestrian uses push-button controls to stop the traffic. The crossing area is shown by studs and a stop line marks the place for drivers to stop when necessary.

Puffin crossings are user-friendly crossings where electronic devices automatically detect when pedestrians are on the crossing. These reduce unnecessary delays in traffic flow.

Toucan crossings are shared by pedestrians and cyclists. Cyclists are permitted to cycle across.

Pelican crossing

The rider and crossings

Some rules and advice apply to all types of crossing:

- you must not park
  - on the crossing; this blocks the way for pedestrians
  - within the area marked by the zigzag lines; this obstructs both the pedestrians' view of approaching vehicles and approaching drivers' view of the crossing
- you must not overtake
  - the moving motor vehicle nearest the crossing
  - the leading vehicle which has stopped to give way to a pedestrian
- even if there are no zigzag lines, never overtake just before a crossing
- give yourself more time to stop if the road is wet or icy

- keep the crossing clear when queueing in traffic; stop before the crossing if you can see that you won't be able to clear it
- you should take extra care where the view of either side of the crossing is blocked by queueing traffic. Pedestrians may be crossing between these vehicles, incorrectly thinking they have stopped to allow them to cross
- always allow pedestrians plenty of time to cross, especially if they are elderly or disabled, and do not harass them by revving your engine or edging forward
- watch out for pedestrians who try to rush across at the last minute.

Puffin crossing

DSA MOTORCYCLE RIDING

Additional rules for different types of crossing

Zebra crossing

Where pedestrians are waiting on the pavement at a zebra crossing and obviously want to cross, slow down and stop to let them cross.

You should stop if you can do so safely, especially

- if anyone is waiting on the pavement with a pram or pushchair
- if children or the elderly are hesitating to cross because of heavy traffic.

You must give way to anyone who

- is already crossing
- has stepped onto the crossing.

Don't wave people across. There could be another vehicle coming in the other direction and you can't be sure what other drivers might do.

Some zebra crossings are divided by a central island. Each half is a separate crossing.

Pelican crossings

These light-controlled crossings have no red and amber before the green. Instead, they have a flashing amber light which means you must give way to pedestrians on the crossing but, if it's clear, you can go on.

Pelican crossings may be

- **straight** a pelican crossing which goes straight across the road is one crossing, even if there is a central refuge. You must wait for people coming from the other side of the refuge
- **staggered** if the crossings on each side of the central refuge are not in line, the crossings are separate.

Puffin crossings

Electronic devices automatically detect when pedestrians are on the crossing and delay the green light until the pedestrians have reached a position of safety. If the pedestrians cross quickly, the pedestrian phase is shortened. If the pedestrians have crossed the road before the phase starts, it will automatically be cancelled.

Because the signals are controlled in this way, there is no flashing amber in the sequence.

Toucan crossings

The signals are push-button operated and there is no flashing amber phase.

Toucan crossing

School crossing patrols

Watch out for the patrols and obey their signals.

At particularly dangerous locations, two amber lights flashing alternately give advance warning of the crossing point.

Don't overtake when you're approaching school crossings and **always** keep your speed down so you're ready to slow down or stop, if necessary.

Defensive riding

Always look well ahead to identify pedestrian crossings early. Look for the flashing yellow beacons, traffic lights, zigzag markings, etc. Use the OSM/PSL routine and keep your speed well down.

Brake lights cannot be seen by the pedestrians at the crossings or oncoming traffic, so if you're the leading vehicle you should consider using an arm signal when you're slowing or stopping.

Tunnels

When approaching a tunnel

- make sure your dipped headlights are on
- stop and remove sunglasses
- observe the road signs and signals
- keep an appropriate distance from the vehicle in front
- switch on your radio and tune to the indicated frequency (if fitted).

If the tunnel is congested

- switch on your hazard warning lights. Only use them for long enough to ensure your warning has been seen
- keep your distance, even if you are moving slowly or stopped
- if possible, listen out for messages on the radio
- follow any instructions given by tunnel officials or variable message signs.

For action to take in the event of a breakdown or accident see page 251.

Parking

The parking rules in *The Highway Code* also apply to motorcycles. When you park, take care to

- park on firm, level ground. On soft ground the stand can sink, causing the machine to fall over. On a very hot day side or centre stands can sink into tarmac softened by the heat. If your machine falls over it could injure a passer-by or damage another parked vehicle
- use the centre stand if you're leaving your machine for some time
- switch off the fuel tap
- lock the steering and take the ignition key with you.

It you park a sidecar outfit on a gradient make sure that it doesn't roll away. Leave the machine in a low gear and block a wheel or wedge it against the kerb.

Motorcycle parking places

In many towns you can find areas set aside for motorcycle parking. These areas often have fixed metal stands to which you can secure your motorcycle.

Some car parks also set aside areas for motorcycles. Look for signs or marked out parking bays.

Security

While theft of motorcycles is all too common, there are steps you can take to make it difficult for thieves:

- if possible park in a car park displaying the 'Secured Car Park' logo. These are car parks that have met the conditions of the police 'Secured Car Parks' scheme. Road signs will indicate their location.
- if parking on the road during the day, park in a busy public place
- at night park in a well lit area
- try not to park in the same place every day
- don't leave your helmet or other possessions with the motorcycle.

When securing your motorcycle always use the steering lock. Additional locking devices include

- high tension steel cable or chain with a high quality padlock
- U-lock
- disc lock.

Fastening your motorcycle to an immovable object or another motorcycle will give extra security.

Other security measures

In addition to locking up your motorcycle you may use other security measures. These include

- fitting an alarm. Make sure the alarm is suitable for your machine. It's a good idea to display a sticker warning that the motorcycle is protected by an alarm - but not the alarm make or model
- having your motorcycle security marked. This involves having the Vehicle Identification Number (VIN) put on the motorcycle. This is unobtrusive and having it put on as many parts as you can will, in the event of theft, help the police to return the motorcycle.

Motorcycle locking devices

Chain lock

U-lock

Disc lock

Modern roads present a huge variety of bends, corners and junctions – points where the road changes direction.

These are often major hazards, and accident statistics show that no rider can afford to venture out without a throrough knowledge of how to deal with them.

The whole of this section is devoted to dealing with bends, corners and junctions safely.

The topics covered

- bends
- negotiating junctions
- turning
- emerging
- lanes at junctions
- types of junctions
  - T-junctions
  - Y-junctions
  - staggered junctions
  - crossroads
  - roundabouts
- dual carriageways.

Bends

Dealing effectively and safely with bends demands that you look well ahead and try to assess accurately how severe the bend is and at what speed you need to be travelling to negotiate it under control.

You should exercise sound judgement and a defensive approach. Where vision is restricted, be prepared to meet

- oncoming vehicles
- obstructions such as broken down or slow moving vehicles
- pedestrians walking on your side of the road.

You should

- control your speed on approach
- choose the right gear for the road speed
- use the throttle carefully
- hold the right line through the bend.

Remember

A bend can feel like a sharp corner to a rider who approaches it too fast – with disastrous results.

Right-hand bends

Keep to the left to improve your view.

Watch out for

- drains
- gravel and road debris
- uneven or slippery surfaces
- drives and entrances
- road junctions
- adverse camber.

When riding around a right-hand bend, don't ride too close to the centre line. Your head might cross over to the other side of the road as you bank over and you may put yourself into the path of oncoming traffic.

Left-hand bends

On a left-hand bend keep to your normal road position. Moving out to the centre of the road as you approach the bend may give you a slightly improved view, but could endanger you by

- placing you too close to the oncoming traffic
- misleading other road users.

The road camber may work to your advantage, but don't go too fast.

Look out for

- pedestrians, especially when there is no footpath
- horse riders
- stationary or broken down vehicles
- oncoming vehicles crossing the centre line
- vehicles waiting to turn right.

Always ride at such a speed that you can stop safely in the distance you can see to be clear.

Speed

Judging the correct road speed as you approach bends and corners takes practice and experience.

The correct speed is the one which takes your motorcycle around the bend under full control with the greatest safety for you, your passenger and other road users.

That speed will depend on the

- type and condition of the road
- sharpness of the bend
- camber of the road
- visibility
- weather conditions.

Camber The camber of a road is the angle at which the road normally slopes away from the centre to help drainage.

On a left-hand bend the camber helps by reducing the angle between the tyre and the road.

On a right-hand bend the opposite is true and the increased angle between tyre and road can lead to reduced stability.

Adverse camber Here the road slopes downwards towards the outside of the corner. The forces acting on your motorcycle could cause reduced stability due to

- the increased angle between tyre and road surface
- the road sloping away from the direction of turn.

Banking On a few bends, such as some motorway slip roads, the road slopes upwards towards the outside of the bend. This applies across the whole width of the road but here traffic is usually restricted to travelling in one direction only.

Left-hand bend: Less angle between tyre and road

Right-hand bend: Greater angle between tyre and road

Adjusting your speed

Don't go into a bend too fast. Reduce speed before you enter the bend.

You can reduce your speed by closing the throttle, and

- allowing the road speed to fall
- using the brakes progressively and, if necessary, changing to a lower gear.

Your speed should be at its lowest as you begin to turn.

Braking on a bend   Avoid braking on a bend.

If you must brake on a bend:

- avoid using the front brake. Rely on the rear brake and engine braking to slow you down. If you must use the front brake, be very gentle. There's a risk of the front tyre losing its grip and sliding sideways
- try to bring your motorcycle upright and brake normally (provided you can do so safely).

Using the throttle

Don't confuse 'using the throttle' with 'accelerating', which means going faster. When dealing with bends 'using the throttle' means using it just enough to make the engine drive the motorcycle around the bend.

The correct speed at a corner or bend will depend on a number of things, including

- how sharp it is
- your view
- road conditions
- whether there is other traffic about.

Taking everything into account, you will have to judge

- the correct position
- the proper speed for the corner or bend
- the gear most suitable for that speed.

The secret of dealing with bends is to make sure that

- your speed is at its lowest before you start the turn
- you use the throttle so that the engine is doing just enough work to drive the motorcycle around the bend without going faster.

Caution

Too much throttle can cause the rear tyre to lose grip and skid.

As you leave the bend and can see further ahead you can increase your speed to suit the road and traffic conditions.

Gears

Make sure you select the correct gear before you enter the bend. The correct gear will depend on a number of factors including

- the speed limit
- road conditions
- other traffic
- warning signs and road markings.

Load

Any change in the centre of gravity or weight the motorcycle is carrying will affect its handling on bends, compared with when it's lightly loaded.

This change may be caused by

- a pillion passenger
- carrying heavy objects
- incorrect tyre pressure.

Negotiating the bend

Look ahead Look well ahead for any indications, such as road signs, warnings and road markings, which will tell you

- the type of bend
- the direction the road takes
- how sharp the bend is
- whether the bend is one of a series.

Assess the situation Ask yourself

- How dangerous does it seem? Remember, the word 'Slow' is usually painted on the road for good reason.
- Are there likely to be obstructions on the bend? For example, slow moving vehicles or parked cars.
- Are there likely to be pedestrians on your side of the road? Is there a footpath?
- What's the camber like? Look well ahead – it's too late to find out in the middle of the bend when your brakes can't help you.

Always ride so you can stop safely within the limit of your vision. Take extra care where your view is restricted.

Approach with care

- As you approach, follow the OSM/PSL routine
- Before you reach the bend
  - take up the best approach position for the type of bend
  - adjust your speed, if necessary, and select the most suitable gear.

Entering the bend As you enter the bend, use the throttle just enough to keep

- the tyres gripping
- full control.

After you begin to turn Avoid braking, except in an emergency

As you go round the bend Keep watching for hazards as the road unfolds and your view improves.

Stopping on a bend

Avoid stopping on a bend, except in an emergency.

If you have to stop, either

- get your motorcycle off the road, or
- stop where following traffic can see you. This is especially important on left-hand bends, where vision can be more limited.

If you can, stop clear of a continuous centre line.

A series of bends

Double and multiple bends are almost always signed. Take note of

- road signs
- double white lines
- arrows warning you to move to the left.

For example, if the second bend followed closely after the first and you haven't taken notice of the road signs or markings, you could find yourself speeding up when you should be slowing down. This can result in hasty replanning and loss of control.

So, on a winding road, use your gears sensibly and select the appropriate gear for the speed. This will enable you to ride at a safe speed while keeping the right amount of load on the engine and maximum grip on the road.

Bends in series often swing in alternate directions. As soon as you have negotiated one, you have to prepare for the next. Look well ahead for changes in the camber of the road, which could affect your control.

At night

On unfamiliar roads, the lights of oncoming traffic may help you to plan ahead. However, negotiating bends at night has its own hazards. Ride with extra care, and

- be prepared for hazards around the bend
- be prepared to be affected by the lights of oncoming traffic, especially on right-hand bends. Don't be taken by surprise
- dip your headlights in advance for oncoming traffic approaching the bend, especially on left-hand bends.

Defensive riding

Always be on the lookout for other vehicles creating dangerous situations. Stay well clear of trouble, such as

- a vehicle overtaking too close to a bend
- a vehicle approaching a bend too fast
- oncoming vehicles straddling the centre lines
- oncoming vehicles skidding in bad weather
- a vehicle waiting to turn into a concealed entrance.

Negotiating junctions

A junction is where two or more roads meet.

Junctions are hazards where there is a greater risk of an accident occurring. Treat them with great care, no matter how easy they look.

There are five main types of junction

- T-junctions
- Y-junctions
- staggered junctions
- crossroads
- roundabouts.

Advance information

Look for information about the junction ahead, and the level of difficulty, such as

- the amount of traffic
- warning signs
- road markings
- direction signs
- 'Give way' and 'Stop' signs
- traffic lights
- a break in the line of buildings
- changes in road surface.

Approaching Junctions

How you approach a junction depends on what you intend to do. You might want to

- cross a major road going ahead
- emerge into a major road by turning right
- emerge into a major road by turning left
- leave a major road by turning right or left into a minor road
- stay on a major road and pass the junction.

A major road is one with priority over another at a junction.

Priority

Usually, road signs and markings indicate priority. Where no priority is shown at a junction, take extra care.

STOP
100 yds

GIVE WAY
50 yds

The junction routine

At every junction use the OSM/PSL routine.

Observation   Look all around so that you're aware of the traffic situation.

Signal   You should signal clearly and in good time.

Manoeuvre   Use the PSL routine:

Position   If the road has no lane markings

- when turning left, keep to the left
- when turning right, keep as close to the centre of the road as is safe. In a one-way street move to the right-hand side of the road in good time.

If the road has lane markings

- use the correct lane for the direction you intend to take
- move into the lane as soon as you can.

Speed   Adjust your speed as necessary.

Look   Watch for other traffic when you reach a point from which you can see.

In traffic, don't

- lose your patience
- switch lanes to gain advantage over others.

When you're moving ahead

- make sure that you're in the correct lane
- look out for vehicles changing lane, either with or without signalling.

Manoeuvre
- Look
- Speed
- Position

Signal
(right-hand
indicator)

Observation

Turning

Turning right into a side road

Assess the junction and use the OSM/PSL routine. Check the road signs and markings.

O – Look in your mirrors and take rear observation as necessary.

S – Signal right in good time.

M – Manoeuvre; use PSL:

P – Position yourself as close to the centre of the road as is safe, so that vehicles can pass on your left.

In a one-way street, keep to the right-hand side of the road.

S – Adjust your **speed** as necessary. Watch out for aproaching traffic. Stop if necessary.

L – Look into the road you're joining. Watch for vehicles waiting to emerge and pedestrians crossing the road.

Take a 'lifesaver' glance over your right shoulder just before you turn. Do this early enough for you to change your plan if it isn't safe to turn.

Avoid cutting the corner. (enter on the left-hand side of the road).

When you've completed the turn

- cancel your signal
- check for following traffic
- accelerate progressively up to the speed suitable for the road and traffic conditions within the set speed limit.

Turning left into a side road

Assess the junction and use the OSM/PSL routine. Check the road signs and markings.

O – **Look** in your mirrors and take rear observation as necessary.

S – **Signal** left at the correct time.

M – **Manoeuvre**; use PSL:

P – Your **position** on approach may not change significantly from your normal riding position but could be affected by factors such as

- parked vehicles or other obstructions
- other road users
- road markings
- the road surface
- the road width.

S – Left turns are often sharper than right turns, so reduce **speed** accordingly.

L – **Look out** for vehicles stopping just before the junction and pedestrians who may not have seen you. Don't overtake a cyclist just before the turn and then cut in just ahead. If you're riding slowly, watch for cyclists coming up on your left.
A 'lifesaver' glance over your left shoulder before you turn may be necessary.

Take special care when

- crossing a bicycle or bus lane
- pedestrians are crossing or waiting to cross, especially children
- on a loose or slippery road surface.

When you've completed the turn

- cancel your signal
- check behind so that you know what's following
- adopt the correct road position
- accelerate progressively up to the speed suitable for the road and traffic conditions within the set speed limit.

Emerging

'Emerging' is when a vehicle leaves one road and joins, crosses or turns into another.

You'll have to judge the speed and distance of any traffic on the road you intend to emerge into, and only continue when it's safe to do so.

This needs care and sometimes patience as well.

When to go

You have to decide when to wait and when it's safe to go. That decision depends largely on your zone of vision.

Your zone of vision is what you can see from your position. It is determined by

- buildings and hedges
- bends in the road or contours in the land
- moving and parked vehicles
- available light and the weather.

As you approach a junction, your zone of vision onto the other road usually improves. The last few feet can be critical.

You can only decide whether to wait or go on when you have put yourself in a position where you can see clearly.

Sometimes parked vehicles interfere with your zone of vision so that you have to inch carefully forward to see more. If another vehicle or a pedestrian is not in your zone of vision, you're not usually in theirs.

Looking means that you need to assess the situation, decide whether it's safe and act accordingly.

After you emerge

- make sure that you cancel your signal
- check behind for the speed and position of other traffic
- accelerate so that your speed is correct for the road and conditions
- keep a safe distance from the vehicle in front.

'Give way' sign or lines

A 'Give way' sign and lines across the road means that you must give way to traffic which is already on the road you intend to enter.

If you can emerge without causing drivers or riders on that road to alter speed or course, you can do so without stopping.

Otherwise, you must stop.

'Stop' sign

You **must always** stop at a 'Stop' sign no matter what the traffic situation seems on the road you intend to enter.

Move off only when

* you have a clear view
* you're sure it's safe.

Junctions without signs or road markings

Treat these with great care.

Don't assume you have priority at an unmarked junction.

Other traffic

Bends and hills could make it more difficult to see traffic coming towards you.

If the vehicle approaching from your right is signalling to turn left into your road, wait until you're sure the vehicle is turning and not just pulling up on the left beyond your road.

Edge forward to improve view

Emerging left into a major road

Assess the junction. Check the road signs and markings. Use the OSM/PSL routine:

O – **Look** in your mirrors and take rear observation as necessary.

S – **Signal** left at the correct time.

M – **Manoeuvre**; use PSL.

P – **Position:** keep to the left.

S – Reduce **speed**. Be prepared to stop. Traffic on a minor road must give way to traffic on a major road.

L – **Look** in all directions at the earliest point from which you can see. Keep looking as you slow down, and stop if necessary.

You must be aware of pedestrians, cyclists and other motorcyclists who may be alongside. You also need to know how traffic behind is reacting to your manoeuvre.

Remember

An approaching vehicle, particularly a bus or a lorry, can easily mask another moving vehicle which may be overtaking.

Emerging right into a major road

Assess the junction. Check road signs and markings. Use the OSM/PSL routine:

O – **Look** in your mirrors and take rear **observation** as necessary.

S – **Signal** right in good time.

M – **Manoeuvre**; use PSL:

P – **Position** yourself as close to the centre of the road as is safe:

- in a one-way street, **position** yourself on the right-hand side of the road

- when turning right it's important to take up your **position** early.

S – Reduce **speed**. Be prepared to stop. You must give way to traffic on a major road.

L – **Look** in all directions at the earliest point from which you can see. Keep looking as you slow down, and stop if necessary.

Watch out for

- traffic turning across your path

- pedestrians.

Lanes at junctions

When you approach a junction

- do so in the correct lane for the direction you intend to take; don't switch lanes to gain advantage
- look well ahead and watch for traffic and direction signs
- look out for signals from vehicles about to change lanes
- look out for vehicles suddenly changing lanes without signalling.

Articulated or long vehicles

Stay clear of large vehicles at junctions. These need much more room than smaller vehicles, and may take up a position that seems incorrect to you.

They often swing out to the right before turning left, and to the left before turning right. At junctions and roundabouts don't be tempted to squeeze past. The rear wheels might cut across your path as the vehicle turns.

Be ready for them to stop if their way is blocked.

Passing minor roads

Look out for road signs indicating minor roads, even if you're not turning off.

Watch out for emerging vehicles. Their view is often obscured at junctions. A vehicle might pull out in front of you.

If this happens, and you're not sure the driver has seen you, slow down. Be prepared to stop.

Be tolerant and don't harass the other driver by sounding your horn aggressively or riding too close.

Remember
Two wrongs don't make a right!

Overtaking

Don't overtake at, or approaching, a junction.

The road surface at junctions

Always watch out for slippery surfaces or loose chippings. Avoid braking while you're turning. Plan ahead: brake before the junction.

Defensive riding

Adjust your overall speed when passing a series of minor roads so you can stop within the distance you can see to be clear.

Types of junctions

Each type of junction can have many variations.

What you intend to do at the junction determines how you approach each type.

T-junctions

You'll find these where a minor road joins a major road from the left or right. The minor road will have either

- a 'Stop' sign and road markings
- a 'Give way' sign and road markings
- give way lines only
- no road signs or markings.

If you're riding on the major road

- take note of any road signs and markings
- watch for vehicles turning or emerging
- avoid overtaking on the approach to a T-junction.

If you're riding on the minor road

- take note of the road signs
- look for slippery surfaces or loose chippings
- stop before emerging if your view into the major road is blocked in any way.

Hatch markings On busier roads, the major road is often split before and after the junction, with a turn-right filter lane protected by white diagonal hatch markings (or chevrons) surrounded by a broken or an unbroken white line.

Join and leave the major road at these junctions exactly as you would a dual carriageway.

Warning

Areas of hatch markings are painted on the road

- to separate streams of traffic
- to protect traffic waiting to turn right.

Where the boundary line is solid, do not enter except in an emergency.

Where the boundary line is broken, you should not ride on these markings unless you can see it's safe to do so.

Remember

Painted road markings can be slippery, especially when wet.

Junctions on bends

Look well ahead for traffic signs and road markings which indicate priority.

These junctions need extra care, especially when turning right from a major road which bends to the left, because

- your field of vision might be limited
- traffic might be approaching at speed from your left
- you'll need time to manoeuvre safely.

Your position before you turn must not endanger either oncoming traffic or yourself.

Wait until there's a gap in the traffic and act positively.

Unmarked junctions

Never assume priority over another road if there are no road signs or markings. What's obvious to you might not be obvious to drivers on the other road.

Watch carefully for vehicles

- approaching the junction on the other road
- waiting at the junction
- emerging from the junction to join or cross your path.

Remember

Any vehicle crossing

- might assume priority and expect you to give way
- might not assume priority, but might have misjudged your speed or not seen you.

Such a vehicle creates a hazard.

You should respond in a safe and sensible manner. Anticipate and adjust your speed accordingly to avoid an accident.

Y-junctions

At a Y-junction the minor road joins the major road at an acute angle. Y-junctions can be deceptive because they often call for little change in direction.

Normally the road going straight ahead has priority and joining roads have either 'Give way' or 'Stop' signs. However, there are many exceptions.

Watch out for oncoming vehicles positioned incorrectly. The drivers might have misjudged the junction.

Going straight ahead on the major road

- Look well ahead for road signs and markings.
- Watch out for vehicles emerging to turn left or right.
- Never overtake when approaching any junction.

Emerging onto the major road

If the angle of approach to the major road is very sharp and from the right, the view to your left might be restricted.

If you position your motorcycle towards the major road at a right angle as you approach the 'Stop' or 'Give way' lines, you will improve your view.

Staggered junctions

These are junctions where roads join from both right and left. At a staggered junction the side roads don't join directly opposite one another but are slightly offset.

If you're riding on the major road look for

- advance warning signs
- vehicles emerging from either side
- traffic turning into the side roads
- vehicles crossing from one minor road into another.

If you're emerging from either minor road

- watch for traffic approaching in both directions
- watch for traffic emerging from the road opposite
- look for slippery surfaces.

If you're crossing from one minor road into another take extra care. If there's room and it's safe, emerge to the centre of the major road. Wait for a safe opportunity to complete the manoeuvre. If there isn't enough room make sure that the gap in the traffic is wide enough in both directions. If in doubt, wait.

Crossroads

Crossroads are often accident blackspots, so take extra care, especially on roads carrying fast moving traffic.

Accidents often involve vehicles turning right.

The procedure when turning at crossroads is much the same as at any other junction.

You'll need to assess the crossroads on approach, so look well ahead and check for road signs and markings which might indicate priority.

Riding on the major road

- Watch for road signs and markings.
- Watch for emerging traffic. Be especially careful of vehicles trying to cut across, using gaps in the traffic. They may misjudge your speed or not see you at all.
- Adjust your speed approaching crossroads.

Turning right

Getting your position and speed correct is vital. Look out for traffic on the road you're joining as well as on the road you're leaving.

Remember a 'lifesaver' glance before starting to turn, especially if you've had to wait.

Turning right when an oncoming vehicle is also turning right

When two vehicles approaching from opposite directions both want to turn right there are two methods that can be used. Either method is acceptable, but will usually be determined by

- the layout of the crossroads
- what course the other driver decides to take
- road markings.

Turning offside to offside

The advantage of this method is that both can see oncoming traffic.

In congested traffic conditions, leave a space for approaching traffic to turn right.

Turning nearside to nearside

This method is less safe because the view of oncoming vehicles is not clear. Watch out for oncoming traffic hidden by larger vehicles and be ready to stop. Police control or road markings sometimes make this method compulsory.

Defensive riding

Try and make eye contact with the driver of the approaching vehicle to determine which course is best. Your speed should allow you to stop if the other driver cuts across your path.

Approaching on a minor road

If you approach the crossroads on one of the minor roads and want to turn onto the major road, as long as the minor road opposite is clear, you should treat it as if you are emerging from a T-junction.

If you want to turn onto the major road, and another vehicle is approaching the crossroads from the minor road opposite, then if you are turning

- left or going straight on, you should proceed with extra caution and make sure no vehicle from the opposite direction is going to cross your path
- right and the other vehicle is going ahead or turning left, you should normally wait for the other vehicle to clear the junction before you make your turn, because you would otherwise be cutting across their path
- right and the other vehicle is turning right, you should try to make eye contact with the other driver to establish who should proceed as neither of you has priority.

Unmarked crossroads

Treat unmarked crossroads with extreme caution since neither road affords priority.

Priority

Never assume you have priority if there are no signs or markings.

Drivers approaching on other roads might also assume they have priority, and an accident could result.

Proceed only when you're sure it's safe to do so.

Remember, you must **look**, **assess** and **decide**, before you **act**.

Take extra care when your view is restricted (by vehicles, walls, hedges, etc.).

Passing side roads

Look out for road signs indicating side roads, even if you aren't turning off. Often views are obscured at urban junctions. A driver may not see you and pull out in front of you.

If you doubt that a driver in a side road has seen you, slow down and sound your horn. Be prepared to stop, if necessary.

Make yourself easy to see. Wear bright clothing and have your headlamp on dipped beam **at all times**.

Parked car

Roundabouts

Roundabouts allow traffic from different roads to merge or cross without necessarily stopping.

Priority

Before you enter a roundabout, you normally give way to any traffic approaching from your immediate right. However, you should keep moving if the way is clear.

In a few cases, traffic on the roundabout has to give way to traffic entering. Look out for 'Give way' signs and road markings on the roundabout.

Some roundabouts have traffic lights (sometimes part-time) which determine priority.

Always use the OSM/PSL routine on approach.

Approaching a roundabout

Always look well ahead for the advance warning sign.

Especially at large or complex roundabouts, this will give you a clear picture of the layout of the roundabout, together with route directions.

The sign will enable you to select the most suitable lane in which to approach the roundabout.

Watch out also for advance warnings of appropriate traffic lanes at the roundabout. These are often backed up by road markings, which usually include route numbers, so

- get into the correct lane in good time
- don't straddle lanes
- never change lanes at the last moment.

Where possible it's a good idea to look across the roundabout and identify the exit you're aiming to take. This will help you to plan the safest course on the roundabout itself.

Procedure

Adopt the following procedure unless road signs or markings indicate otherwise:

Going left

- Indicate left as you approach.
- Approach in the left-hand lane.
- Keep to that lane on the roundabout.
- Maintain a left turn signal through the roundabout.

Going ahead

- No signal is necessary on approach.
- Approach in the left-hand lane. If you can't use the left-hand lane because, for example, it's blocked, use the next lane to it.
- Keep to the selected lane on the roundabout.
- Take rear observation especially to the nearside.
- Indicate left after you have passed the exit just before the one you intend to take.
- If you have to cross a lane on your left to reach your exit take a 'lifesaver' glance to the nearside before changing direction.

Going right or full circle

- Indicate right as you approach.
- Approach in the right-hand lane.
- Keep to that lane and maintain the signal on the roundabout.
- Take rear observation especially to the nearside.
- Indicate left after you have passed the exit just before the one you intend to take.
- If you have to cross a lane on your left to reach your exit take a 'lifesaver' glance to the nearside before changing direction.

Remember

When using the right-hand lane to go ahead or when turning right, be aware of traffic in the lane to your left.

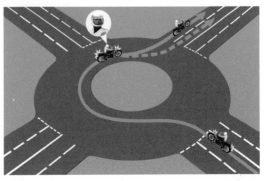

More than three lanes

Where there are more than three lanes at the approach to the roundabout, use the most appropriate lane on approach and through the roundabout, unless road signs or markings tell you otherwise.

Defensive riding

Always keep an eye on the vehicle in front as you're about to enter the roundabout.

Don't assume the driver won't have to stop while you're still looking to the right. Many rear end collisions happen this way. Make sure the vehicle has actually moved away.

Hazards

Roundabouts can be particularly hazardous areas. While negotiating the roundabout you should be especially aware of

- pedestrians: in many areas, zebra crossings are located near the entrances and exits to roundabouts. Even if there are no formal crossings, pedestrians may attempt to cross the road at these junctions. Always be aware of pedestrians who may be trying to cross the road

- cyclists and horseriders: they often keep to the outside of the roundabout even when intending to turn right. Take extra care and allow them plenty of room

- long vehicles: because of their length, they might take a different course as they approach the roundabout and as they go round it. Watch out for their signals and allow for the rear of their vehicle cutting in

- all vehicles: be prepared for vehicles to cross your path to leave at the next exit. Always be on the lookout for their signals

- road surface:
    - this can become polished and slippery
    - fuel spillage. As vehicles travel around roundabouts fuel can spill onto the road. In wet weather this can be seen as a rainbow coloured pattern across the road.

  In wet weather a polished road surface and/or spilt fuel can make the road very slippery.

Mini roundabouts

- approach these in the same way as a roundabout, but remember, there's less space to manoeuvre and less time to signal. For example, there's often insufficient time to signal left when leaving
- vehicles coming towards you might want to turn right. Give way to them
- be sure any vehicle on the roundabout is going to leave it before you join it
- beware of drivers who are using the roundabout for a U-turn
- you must pass round the central markings.

Double mini roundabouts

- treat each roundabout separately and give way to traffic from your right
- take careful all-round observation before you enter.

Multiple roundabouts

At some complex junctions, a large roundabout can incorporate a series of mini roundabouts at the intersections.

You need to take extra care because traffic can be travelling in all directions around the large roundabout.

Look and assess   Keep a good look out and assess the situation at each mini roundabout. Look for

*   direction signs
*   lane markings

well in advance.

Dual carriageways

These are roads which have a central reserve dividing streams of traffic. There may also be a safety barrier on the central reserve.

Although some dual carriageways appear similar to motorways, the same regulations don't apply.

Beware of slow moving vehicles such as farm tractors, cyclists and pedestrians.

Turning left onto a dual carriageway

If there's no acceleration lane or slip road

• emerge as you would to turn left on a single carriageway

Remember

Traffic may be travelling faster than on a single carriageway.

If there's an acceleration lane or slip road

• emerge as you would to join a motorway
• use the acceleration lane to increase speed. Match your speed with that of traffic in the left-hand lane
• move into a safe gap in the traffic.

Remember to use a 'lifesaver' glance just before you move into the left lane.

Turning left from a dual carriageway

If there's no deceleration lane or slip road

• signal your intentions clearly and in good time
• slow down in good time.

If there's a deceleration lane or slip road

• signal in good time
• don't reduce speed until you've moved into the deceleration lane
• check your speedometer. If you've been riding at high speeds you may find yourself travelling faster than you realise.

Turning right onto a dual carriageway

You'll have to cross the first carriageway before you can join the carriageway you want.

If the central reserve is wide enough

- you can wait in it for a gap in the traffic on the carriageway you want

- don't leave yourself jutting out either side of the central reserve.

If the central reserve is too narrow, wait until the dual carriageway is clear in both directions.

Remember

Traffic may be travelling at high speeds. If in doubt, wait for a large gap in the traffic.

Turning right from a dual carriageway

The central reserve sometimes has gaps for turning right. These may have special filter lanes.

To turn right, use your mirrors and signal in good time. Don't forget a 'lifesaver' glance before you turn.

You may have to cross the path of fast oncoming vehicles in two or more lanes. If in doubt, wait.

Defensive riding is based on good observation and anticipation.

On today's roads it's important that you look and plan well ahead. Avoid putting yourself in a situation where you're trying to do too many things at once.

Question the intentions of other road users and try to anticipate their actions. Anticipation is a skill which develops with experience. This part describes the main features of defensive riding which will help you to gain that experience safely. Use these techniques whenever you ride.

The topics covered

- defensive riding
- observation
- hazards
- lighting conditions
- other road users.

Defensive riding

Defensive riding is based on effective observation, good anticipation and control. It's about always questioning the actions of other road users and being prepared for the unexpected, so as not to be taken by surprise.

Defensive riding involves

- awareness
- planning
- anticipating
- staying in control

and riding with

- responsibility
- care
- consideration and courtesy.

It means putting safety above all else.

It's about having real concern, not only for your own safety, but also for other road users, including the most vulnerable.

Expect other people to make mistakes, and be ready to slow down or stop – even if you think you have the right of way.

Never rely on other road users doing the correct thing.

Your safety

Your safety lies mainly in your own hands. The better your control of your motorcycle and road space, the safer you'll be.

A good example

Your riding should always set a good example to other road users.

You never know when your good example will make a deep impression on another rider, especially a learner or inexperienced rider, and perhaps save lives in the future.

Reducing hostility

With defensive riding, you show patience and anticipation. This helps to reduce the number of incidents which result in

- open hostility
- abusive language
- threats
- physical violence.

Avoid the kind of riding that

- gives offence to other road users
- provokes reaction
- creates dangerous situations.

Competitive riding

Never ride in a spirit of competition.

Competitive riding is, inherently, the opposite of defensive riding. It increases the risks to everyone.

Observation

When you take rear observation, just looking is not enough. You must act sensibly on what you see.

You must make a mental note of the

- speed
- behaviour
- possible intentions

of any other road user.

If you're not observing effectively, you can't assess a traffic situation correctly.

At junctions, there's no point in just looking if your view is obstructed – for example, by parked vehicles. You must also move carefully into a position where you can see without emerging into the path of oncoming traffic.

- **Look**
- **Assess** and
- **Decide** before you
- **Act.**

That's what effective observation is all about.

Observing what's ahead

A skilful rider constantly watches and interprets what's happening ahead.

Do

Always ride at such a speed that you can stop safely within the distance you can see to be clear.

A good rider will constantly scan the road ahead and to the side and, by use of effective rear observation, be aware of the situation behind.

Approaching a bend   Ask yourself:

- can I see the full picture?
- how sharply does it bend?
- am I in the right position?
- is my speed right?
- what might I meet?
- could I stop if I had to?

Approaching a junction   Ask yourself:

- have I seen the whole junction?
- can others see me?
- am I sure they've seen me?
- have I got an escape route if they haven't?

Don't

Ride beyond the limits of your vision.

Zone of vision at a junction

Your zone of vision is what you can see as you look forward and to the side from your position. As you approach a junction, your zone of vision onto the other road usually improves.

You may need to get very close before you can look far enough into another road to see if it's safe to proceed. The last few feet are often critical.

Sometimes parked vehicles restrict your view so much that you need to stop and inch forward for a proper view before you emerge.

- Look in every direction before you emerge.
- Keep looking as you join the other road.
- Be ready to stop.
- Use all the information available to you – look through the windows of parked vehicles.
- Use the reflections in shop windows to observe oncoming traffic.

Screen pillar obstruction The windscreen pillars can cause obstructions to a driver's view of the road. You should be aware of this effect, particularly when emerging from junctions.

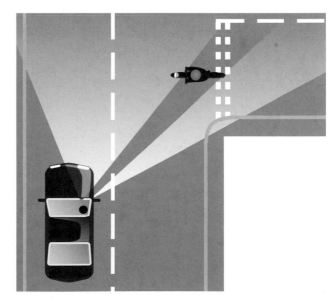

Other road users It can be difficult to see some other road users, especially when you are emerging from a junction. Those who are particularly at risk are

- pedestrians; they frequently cross at a junction and often find it difficult to judge the speed and course of approaching traffic

- cyclists; they can be difficult to see, because they can easily be obscured by trees and other objects, especially if they are riding close to the side of the road. They might be approaching at a higher speed than you expect

- other motorcyclists; like cyclists, they are often less easy to see than other motor vehicles.

Remember

Never rely solely on a quick glance – give yourself time to take in the whole scene.

If another vehicle or a pedestrian is not in your zone of vision, you're not usually in theirs.

Making eye contact with other road users helps you to judge whether they have seen you.

Being seen

As you approach a junction where you can see a vehicle waiting to emerge, ask yourself:

- Has the driver seen me?
- What if I haven't been seen?

Many collision accidents happen at road junctions when a driver doesn't see a motorcyclist.

Daytime use of dipped headlamps and wearing bright clothing increase your chances of being seen. Improving your visibility is an important aspect of defensive riding.

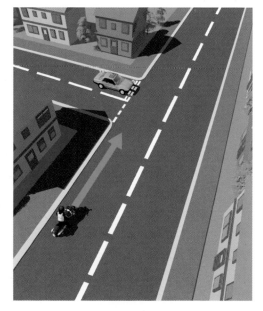

Observing traffic behind you

You should always know as much as you can about the traffic behind you.

Before you move off, change direction or change speed, you must know how your action will affect other road users.

You must also be aware of traffic likely to overtake.

When should you take rear observation?

Well **before** you signal your intention or make any manoeuvre. For example, before

- moving off
- changing direction
- turning right or left
- overtaking
- changing lanes
- slowing or stopping.

(See Part eight, 'Rear observation')

Just looking is not enough! You must act sensibly on what you see, and take note of the speed, behaviour and possible intentions of traffic behind.

Another road user's blind spot Avoid riding in another road user's blind spot for any longer than necessary.

Approaching green traffic lights

Ask yourself:

- how long have they been on green?
- are there many vehicles already waiting at either side of the junction? (If there's a queue, the lights are probably about to change)
- do I have time to stop?
- can the vehicle behind me stop? If it's a large goods vehicle, it might need a greater distance to pull up.

Don't

- try to beat the traffic signals by accelerating
- leave it until the last moment to brake – harsh braking causes skids.

Remember

Another driver might anticipate the change of signals by accelerating away while the lights are still showing red and amber.

A combination of these actions often results in a collision that could be avoided.

Traffic signals not working

Where traffic signals are not working, treat the situation as you would an unmarked junction and **proceed with great care.**

Hazards

A hazard is any situation which could involve adjusting speed or changing course. To identify a hazard, you must look well ahead for clues such as

- road signs
- changes in road conditions
- parked vehicles
- junctions
- cyclists
- other motorcyclists
- pedestrians
- horse riders
- animals, particularly dogs off the lead.

Remember, as soon as you've recognised a hazard, you must use the mirrors or look behind to assess

- how other road users will affect your planning
- how your actions will affect following traffic.

Allowing time and space

Always leave yourself enough time and space to cope with what's ahead.

- keep your eyes scanning the far and near distance, especially in towns, where things change quickly
- check regularly on what's following you
- watch for clues about what's going to happen next.

For example, a parked car could spell danger if the driver is sitting in it, or you see vapour from the exhaust in cold weather. This could indicate that

- a door might open suddenly
- the car might pull out without warning.

If you can see underneath a parked vehicle, and you can see feet at the other side, a pedestrian might appear suddenly.

Effective observation and anticipation are your main defences.

Separation distances

Always keep a good separation distance between you and the vehicle in front.

Leave a gap of at least one metre or yard for each mph of your speed, or use the two-second rule (see Part eight, 'Separation distance').

In bad conditions, leave at least double the distance or a four-second time gap.

Tailgating   When a vehicle behind is too close to you, ease off very gradually and increase the gap between you and the vehicle in front.

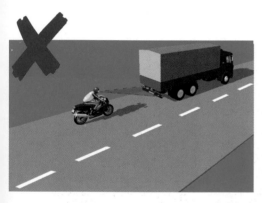

Large vehicles   Take extra care when following large vehicles, especially at roundabouts, junctions, entrances, etc.

The driver might have to take a course that seems incorrect to you. For example, moving out to the right before turning left.

Keep well back from any large vehicles that are in the process of manoeuvring to the left or right.

Don't get caught out by trying to pass on the left.

Large vehicles can also block your view. Your ability to see and plan ahead will be improved if you keep back.

Remember

If you are following too close behind a large vehicle, the driver might not be able to see you in the mirrors.

Recognising hazards

Events can happen at the same time, or in quick succession.

In the illustration, the rider must pull out to pass the stationary van, but

- is the blue car really going to turn left? (The driver might have forgotten to cancel the indicator from a previous turn)
- if the blue car does turn, will the pedestrian decide to cross?
- when will the rider see the red car, which may want to turn left?

If you're travelling too fast, you're not likely to be able to cope with all the events at once.

The action you need to take will vary from one hazard to another. Any action which involves a change of speed or course is called a manoeuvre.

A manoeuvre can vary from slowing slightly to turning on a very busy road.

Remember

The defensive rider is always

- in the correct position
- travelling at the correct speed for the road, traffic and weather conditions
- in the right gear
- anticipating and prepared for the next change in the traffic situation.

Country roads

These roads present their own hazards. Take extra care and reduce your speed as you approach bends and junctions.

Bends and junctions Bends can often be sharper than you think they are going to be. They may also obscure other, more vulnerable road users, such as pedestrians, horse riders and cyclists, or larger slow moving farm vehicles.

Junctions, especially minor junctions or entrances to farm premises, are not always signed and may be partially hidden.

Road surfaces On country roads be prepared to find

- worn road surfaces
- mud
- hedge cuttings
- leaves in the autumn.

If you see mud or hedge cuttings on the road, anticipate finding the cause around the next bend. This may be farm machinery or farm animals. Either way it will be a slow moving hazard and you need to be prepared to stop.

Other road users There are often no pavements or footpaths on the side of the road in country areas. Where there aren't any, pedestrians are advised to walk on the right-hand side of the road so they can see oncoming traffic. You should be prepared to find people walking or jogging on your side of the road.

Horse riders and cyclists are often found on country roads. Give them plenty of space and always be patient and wait until it is safe before overtaking, especially on narrow or winding roads.

Approaching any hazard

Follow the OSM/PSL routine every time you recognise a hazard:

- **O**bservation
- **S**ignal
- **M**anoeuvre.

Observation Check the position of following traffic using your mirrors or by looking behind at an appropriate time.

Signal If necessary, signal your intention to change course or slow down. Signal clearly and in good time.

Manoeuvre Carry out the manoeuvre if it's still safe to do so. Manoeuvre has three phases:

- **P**osition
- **S**peed
- **L**ook.

Position Get into the correct position in good time to negotiate the hazard. This helps other road users to anticipate what you intend to do.

Positioning yourself too late can be dangerous.

Ask yourself:

- can I see and be seen?
- are other vehicles restricting my course of action?
- have I enough room to get out of any difficulties?

Avoid cutting in front of other drivers or riders.

If lanes are closed or narrow because of road works, move into the correct lane in good time.

Speed Ask yourself:

- could I stop in time if the vehicle in front suddenly brakes sharply?
- am I going too fast for the road conditions?
- am I in the right gear needed to keep control?

Be prepared to slow down as you approach a hazard.

Always be ready to stop.

Look Keep looking ahead to assess all possible dangers.

This is particularly important at a junction.

Look in all directions, even if you're not turning.

If you're joining a road, keep looking as you turn from one road to the other.

Watch out for

- traffic turning across your path
- pedestrians.

Lighting conditions

In the dark, seeing hazards is more difficult. The clues are there, but you have to pick them out. Look for

- illuminated road signs
- reflective road signs
- reflectors between white lines
- the glow of vehicle headlights on buildings, trees and hedges indicating bends and junctions.

In the dark

- it can be difficult to judge distances and speed from headlights
- headlights on vehicles make it difficult to see pedestrians, cyclists and any vehicle with dim lights
- don't let shop and advertising lights distract you
- watch for zebra crossings, traffic lights and road signs.

Wet roads

Wet roads increase reflected and distracting light. The reflections from wet surfaces make it more difficult to see unlit objects.

The combination of rain and darkness reduces visibility further. On unlit or poorly lit roads keep your speed down. Remember, your stopping distance will be increased while your visibility is reduced.

Road surfaces

Stay alert to the road surface ahead because you might have to brake.

A wet road means

- less efficient braking
- a longer distance needed to stop
- a greater risk of skidding.

Ride more slowly on a wet road, and take extra care.

Unlit side view

When you're sideways on to other road users you'll be less easily seen, for example when

- passing side turnings
- emerging right or left.

Wearing reflective material will help passing drivers to see you.

Other road users

Cyclists

Make allowances for cyclists. They have every right to be on the road. Allow them plenty of room.

The younger the cyclist, the more you must watch them.

Cyclists might

- glance round, showing they might be about to move out or turn
- make sudden sideways movements into your path
- be carrying objects which may affect their control and balance
- weave about, slow down, or stop and get off on a hill
- swerve round potholes or inspection covers
- have problems in bad weather, particularly strong crosswinds
- find difficulties on poor road surfaces or where tramlines are set in the road.

Powered vehicles used by disabled people

These small vehicles can be used on the pavement and on the road. They are extremely vulnerable when they are on the road because of

- their small size, especially their low height
- their low speed (they have a maximum speed of 8 mph).

They are often not easy to see. On a dual carriageway they will have an amber flashing light, but on other roads you may not have that advance warning.

Buses and coaches

Look well ahead when you see buses and coaches at a bus stop. Be aware of

- people getting off the bus or coach and not looking properly before they cross the road (even if they look, their view is often restricted)
- buses and coaches pulling away from the bus stop. If they are signalling to move out, always give way to them if you can do so safely.

Pedestrians

When turning from one road to another

- always look out for pedestrians
- give way to any who are crossing
- take extra care if a pedestrian fails to look your way as you approach.

Pedestrian crossings

Never overtake on the approach to pedestrian crossings.

Elderly persons

Several factors make elderly persons more vulnerable.

Poor eyesight or hearing might mean they are not aware of approaching traffic. They might not be able to judge the speed of approaching traffic when crossing the road. Even when they do realise the danger, they may be unable to move quickly, or they may become flustered.

They may also take longer to cross the road. Be patient and do not hurry them by revving your engine or edging forwards.

Disabled pedestrians   Take special care with visually impaired or disabled people.

Remember that a person with hearing difficulty is not easy to identify.

Visually impaired people may carry a white cane or use a guide dog. Those who are deaf and blind may carry a white cane with a red band.

Children   Take extra care where children might be about, particularly in residential areas and near schools and parks.

Be aware that a school crossing warden may stop you to escort children across a busy road.

Children are impulsive and often unpredictable. Therefore, ride slowly in narrow roads where parked cars obscure your view.

Look out for parked ice cream vans. Children are more interested in ice cream than they are in traffic, and they may run into the road unexpectedly.

Animals

Animals are easily frightened by noise and vehicles coming close to them.

You should

- ride slowly and quietly; don't sound the horn
- keep engine speed low; don't rev your engine
- always watch out for animals on unfenced roads.

Give animals as much room as possible.

Persons in charge of animals If someone in charge of animals signals to you to stop, do so and stop your engine.

Guide dogs A guide dog for a visually handicapped person usually has a distinctive loop type of harness. Remember, the dog is trained to wait if there's a vehicle nearby.

For a person with hearing difficulty, the guide dog usually has a distinctive orange lead and collar.

Horse riders Be particularly careful when approaching horses, especially those ridden by children. Always pass wide and slow and look out for signals given by the riders.

Watch the behaviour of the horses. The riders might be having difficulty controlling them.

Take special care when meeting what appears to be a riding-school group. Many of the riders might be inexperienced.

Always treat horses as potential hazards and take great care when meeting or passing them.

Remember

Always think of the other road user, not just of yourself.

Please slow down!

Motorways are designed to help traffic move quickly and safely over long distances. They place demands on both the rider and machine that are different from those of other roads. For example, the effect of weather conditions can be exaggerated by higher speeds.

High-speed riding means that situations can develop rapidly so you need to be alert and feeling well. Use the two-second rule and look well ahead. Don't just focus on the vehicle in front.

On a motorway you'll find that you're exposed to wind turbulence, particularly from larger vehicles. Anticipate the wind effect and make sure that you keep full control of your machine.

The topics covered

- riding on motorways
- motorway signs and signals
- joining the motorway
- on the motorway
- lane discipline
- overtaking
- leaving a motorway
- motorway weather conditions
- stopping on motorways
- roadworks.

Riding on motorways

You must make sure your motorcycle is safe and in good working order.

Motorways must not be used by

- pedestrians
- cyclists
- horse riders
- holders of provisional car and motorcycle licences.

In addition the following vehicles must not be used on the motorway:

- motorcycles under 50 cc
- certain slow moving vehicles with oversized loads – except with special permission
- most invalid carriages
- agricultural vehicles.

Due to the demanding nature of motorways, make sure that

- you have a thorough knowledge of the sections of the *The Highway Code* dealing with motorways
- you know and understand the motorway warning signs and signals
- you feel fit and alert to ride. Never use the motorway if you feel tired or unwell
- you never park except at service areas. If you need to rest, you'll sometimes have to travel long distances before an exit or a service area. Remember, it's an offence to stop on the hard shoulder, an exit or a slip road, unless in an emergency.

Being seen on a motorway

Because of the higher speeds, it's important that you can be seen easily by other drivers. Wear high-visibility clothing and ride with your headlamp on dipped beam.

The motorcycle on the motorway

High speeds and long distances increase the risk of mechanical failure.

You should carry out the following checks:

- **tyres** – they must be in good condition and with the correct pressure. Follow the guidance given in the owner's handbook which often tells you the different pressures to be used when carrying a passenger or load
- **instruments** – make sure there are no faults
- **warning lights** – make sure each is working correctly
- **mirrors** (if fitted) – make sure they are clean and correctly positioned
- **lights and indicators** – make sure they are all working correctly.

Also make sure that

- your brakes can stop you safely
- your steering is in good order.

For safety, convenience and good vehicle care you should also check the following items:

- **fuel** – make sure you have enough fuel to avoid running out between service areas
- **oil** – high speeds may mean your engine uses oil
- **water** (liquid cooled engines) – higher speeds can mean a warmer engine, especially in traffic tailbacks in hot weather.

Make sure any load is secure   Check that everything carried on your motorcycle or trailer is safe and secure.

If anything should fall from your motorcycle or from another vehicle, stop on the hard shoulder and use the emergency telephone to inform the police.

Never try to retrieve it yourself.

Motorway signs and signals

Signs

Leading to the motorway Direction signs from ordinary roads to the motorway have white lettering and figures on a blue panel, often bordered in white.

These signs may

*   stand alone
*   be included in other larger signs of various colours.

On the motorway You may find the following types of sign on the motorway:

*   advance direction signs
*   countdown markers
*   signs giving information about service areas
*   signs with a brown background indicating tourist attractions which can be reached by leaving at the next exit.

All these signs are very much larger than those on ordinary roads because you need to be able to see them from a distance. This is a good reminder that you must leave more room for all manoeuvres on motorways.

Each junction has an identifying number which corrresponds with current road maps, to help you plan your route and know where you need to leave the motorway.

Speed limit signs

*   Signs which display a speed limit within a red ring indicate mandatory maximum speed limits. You must obey these signs. If you don't, you risk prosecution.
*   Black and white rectangular signs recommend maximum speed limits which you should observe.

Signals

Signals will warn of dangers ahead, such as

- accidents
- fog
- icy roads.

Flashing amber lights   Look out for flashing amber lights and signs either on the central reservation or overhead. These warn you of

- lane closures
- roadworks
- other hazards.

They might also show a temporary advisory speed limit, so

- slow down to the speed limit
- be ready to slow down still more to pass the obstacle or danger
- look out for police signs
- don't speed up until you see the sign ending the temporary restriction (or there are no more flashing amber lights).

Red lights   Some signs have flashing red lights as well.

A red light (it may be a red 'X') warns you that you must not go beyond the red light in that lane, so

- start to slow down in good time
- be ready to change lanes.

If the red light flashes on a slip road, you must not enter it.

If a red light flashes on the central reservation or at the side of the road, you must not go beyond the signal in **any** lane.

Joining a motorway

At an entry point where a slip road leads to the motorway, adjust your speed to that of the traffic already on the motorway before joining it.

Give priority to traffic already on the motorway.

Join where there's a suitable gap in the left-hand lane.*

Use the OSM/PSL routine.

A 'lifesaver' glance will verify the position of other vehicles. Try to avoid stopping at the end of the slip road unless queuing to join other slow moving traffic.

Do

- indicate your intention to join the motorway
- make sure you can be seen
- assess the speed of the traffic on the motorway before you try to merge in.

Don't

- force your way into the traffic stream
- ride along the hard shoulder.

Once you've joined the motorway, keep in the left-hand lane* until you've had time to judge and adjust to the speed of the traffic already on the motorway.

*In a very few cases, the lane merges from the right. Take extra care when joining or meeting traffic at these locations.

When other vehicles join the motorway

After you pass an exit, there's usually an entrance where other vehicles can join:

- don't try to race them while they're on the slip road
- look well ahead if there are several vehicles joining the motorway – be prepared to adjust your speed
- if it's safe, move to another lane to make it easier for joining traffic to merge.

On the motorway

Continually reassess the movement of the vehicles

- directly ahead (in the near and far distance)
- alongside you
- behind you.

At high speeds, situations change rapidly. Effective observation helps you prepare for any sudden developments.

For example, an increase in the number of vehicles ahead could mean that traffic is slowing down and 'bunching', or a flashing breakdown light will warn you to slow down until you're sure of what's happening.

If you see serious congestion ahead, you can use hazard warning lights (if fitted) briefly to alert drivers behind you. This can reduce the risk of rear-end collisions, especially in bad weather.

Keeping your distance

The faster the traffic, the more time and space you need.

You must

- give yourself greater margins than on ordinary roads
- make sure there's enough space between you and the vehicle ahead.

Traffic normally travels faster because there are usually no

- ordinary junctions
- sharp bends*
- roundabouts*
- steep hills
- traffic lights

- slow moving vehicles

*Some motorway links, where motorway regulations also apply, have roundabouts and sharp bends.

How big a gap? Leave a gap of at least one metre or yard for each mph of your speed.

A useful method of judging this is to use the two-second rule described in Part eight under 'Separation distance'.

This rule is reinforced on some motorways where there are chevrons painted on the carriageway. Keep at least two chevrons between you and the vehicle in front.

Adverse weather Leave at least double the space if the road is wet or slippery.

Obstructions

If vehicles ahead switch on their hazard warning lights be prepared for slow moving or stationary traffic.

Look well ahead and leave yourself plenty of room. Check behind to see how the following traffic is reacting.

If you find yourself catching up with slower moving traffic there could be an obstruction ahead. Be aware that other vehicles may be slowing gradually without the need to brake. You won't have warning from their brake lights in these situations.

Lane discipline

Lane discipline is vitally important on motorways. You should normally ride in the left-hand lane:

- don't change lanes unless you need to
- ride in the centre of the lane
- don't wander into another lane.

Changing lanes on a motorway

Always use the OSM/PSL routine well before you intend to change lanes.

At higher speeds, you must start the routine much earlier.

Look, and if necessary, signal in good time. Remember vehicles might come up behind very quickly.

The sooner you indicate, the sooner other drivers are warned of your intended movement. They'll expect a change in the traffic pattern and have time to prepare for it.

Two-lane discipline

On a two-lane motorway, the correct position is in the left-hand lane.

The right-hand (offside) lane is for overtaking and once you have overtaken you should return to the left-hand lane as soon as it is safe to do so.

Large goods vehicles are permitted to use either lane.

Three- or four-lane discipline

Because of the volume of traffic on three-lane motorways, many are being widened to four or more lanes in each direction.

Keep to the left-hand lane unless there are a great many slower vehicles ahead.

Avoid repeatedly changing lane – it's possible to stay in the centre or outer lanes while you are overtaking a number of slower moving vehicles, but don't stay in these lanes

• longer than you have to

• if you are delaying traffic behind you.

Drivers of large goods vehicles, buses, coaches or any vehicle towing a trailer are not allowed to use the extreme right-hand lane of a motorway with more than two lanes, unless one or more lanes are temporarily closed.

Don't stay in an overtaking lane longer than it takes you to move out, overtake and move in again safely. Make sure you don't block traffic which is not allowed to use the outer lane.

Remember

The right hand lane is for overtaking - it's not the 'fast lane'.

Crawler and climbing lanes

A steep hill on a motorway might have a crawler or climbing lane to avoid heavy vehicles slowing down the flow of traffic.

Overtaking

Leave a safe distance between you and the vehicle you intend to overtake.

Use the appropriate parts of the OSM/PSL routine. For example:

Observation   Check behind to verify the speed, course and position of following traffic.

Position   Position yourself so that you can see well past the vehicle in front.

Speed   Make sure you're going fast enough or can accelerate quickly enough to overtake without blocking any vehicle coming up behind.

Look   Look ahead and behind to check if there's anything preventing you from overtaking safely. For example, a lane closure ahead, or traffic coming up much faster from behind in the right-hand lane.

Try to anticipate if the vehicle ahead will move out to overtake.

Remember

- **Look**
- **Assess** well ahead
- **Decide** – don't rush
- **Act** – but only when you're sure it's safe.

Observation

Remember that vehicles coming up in the right-hand lane are likely to be moving faster than you are.

Be on the look out for vehicles returning to the lane you intend to use.

Signal

You must signal well before you start to move out. This gives drivers behind you plenty of time to anticipate what you intend to do and could influence any manoeuvres they're planning.

Pulling out

Take a 'lifesaver' glance into the blind spot before moving out smoothly into an overtaking lane.

Cancel your signal.

Overtake as quickly and safely as possible.

As you overtake a large goods vehicle, bus or coach expect to be buffeted by the changing air pressure. Don't ride too close to the vehicle you're overtaking.

Moving back left

Pass the vehicle and move back into the left as soon as you're sure it's safe to do so.

Don't cut in too soon in front of the vehicle you've just passed.

Look for any vehicles about to move out into the lane you intend to move into.

On busy motorways

If you come up behind traffic moving more slowly than you are when you're overtaking, be patient and don't

- intimidate the driver ahead by repeatedly flashing your headlight and riding dangerously close behind
- filter between fast moving lanes of traffic.

Overtaking on the left

Never overtake on the left, unless

- the traffic is moving in queues and
- the queue on your right is moving more slowly than the queue you are in.

Ride defensively

Let faster traffic pass you.

Don't move to a lane on the left to overtake.

Never use the hard shoulder to overtake – unless directed to do so by traffic signs at road works, or by police officers.

Leaving a motorway

Unless you're going to the end of the motorway, you'll leave by moving left from the left-hand lane into the slip road. Get into that lane in plenty of time.

Plan well ahead, particularly on three- or four-lane motorways.

Road signs

Use the road signs and markers to help you time your exit and use your mirrors and indicators appropriately.

You'll have plenty of time to observe the signs and markers so there's no need to rush.

On a three- or four-lane motorway, this could mean changing lanes more than once, and you should follow the OSM routine for each change of lane.

One mile before the exit   A junction sign with road numbers, unless there are exits very close together.

Half a mile before the exit   A sign with the names of places accessible from that exit.

From 270 metres (300 yards) before the exit   Countdown markers at 270 metres (300 yards), 180 metres (200 yards) and 90 metres (100 yards) before the start of the slip road.

Do

use your mirrors and signal left in good time to move into the left-hand lane.

Don't

• move to the left more than one lane at a time

• cut across at the last moment, especially from the second lane of a three- or four-lane motorway.

Occasionally, where motorways merge, there may be an exit just prior to the one you intend to take. In these cases, or where there are service areas near to exits, look well ahead for the advance warning signs.

If you miss your exit, carry on to the next exit.

End of motorway

There will be 'End of motorway' signs at all exits. These mean that the road you're joining will have different rules.

Remember to watch for any signs telling you what these are, particularly

- speed limits
- dual carriageway
- two-way traffic
- clearway
- motorway link road
- part-time traffic lights.

Speed when leaving a motorway

After riding at motorway speeds for some time, your judgement of speed will almost certainly be affected: 40 or 45 mph seems more like 20 mph.

- Adjust your riding to suit the new conditions.
- Check your speedometer. It will give you the accurate speed.

Motorway slip roads and link roads often have sharp curves which should be taken at much lower speeds. The road surface on these curves may be slippery – look for signs of fuel spillage.

Motorway weather conditions

When you ride on motorways the most common weather problems will be

- crosswinds
- rain
- fog.

Crosswinds

A sudden gust of wind can blow you off course. Keep your speed down where there is a danger of crosswinds. Riding more slowly will help you to keep control. You need to be especially careful

- as you come out from the shelter of a large vehicle when overtaking or being overtaken
- on exposed stretches.

In strong wind, drivers of high-sided vehicles, or those towing caravans, are also likely to experience difficulties. Allow for this when riding near these vehicles.

CROSSWIND

CROSSWIND

Drop in pressure can pull rider towards large vehicle

Rain

In heavy rain the surface spray from other vehicles, especially large ones, will seriously reduce visibility, as well as increase stopping distance. Make sure that

- you're visible. Use dipped headlights and wear bright clothing
- you can see clearly. Keep your visor or goggles clean
- you adjust your speed to suit the conditions and leave larger separation distances, at least double the normal.

Fog

In fog you need to

- slow down and keep your distance from the vehicle ahead
- use dipped headlamps and rear fog lamps (if fitted) when visibility falls below 100 metres (about 330 feet)
- make sure that your visor or goggles are clean and aren't hindering your view ahead
- wear bright clothing. This will help other drivers to see you.

Fog can drift quickly and is often patchy.

If a motorway warning sign shows 'Fog'

- be prepared
- reduce speed in good time.

Stopping on motorways

You must only stop on a motorway if

- it's an emergency
- it will prevent an accident
- police or road signs or signals indicate that you must.

If you need to stop for a rest, find a service area. The hard shoulder is for emergencies only. It isn't for parking or resting.

Breakdowns

If your motorcycle breaks down, try to get onto the hard shoulder.

When you have stopped

- park as far to the left as you can away from the traffic
- switch on hazard warning lights if fitted
- switch on your parking lights in poor visibility or at night
- make your way to the nearest emergency telephone and call for assistance.

Never attempt even minor repairs.

Emergency telephones   Police-controlled emergency telephones are on most stretches of motorway at one mile intervals.

Look for a telephone symbol and arrows on marker posts 100 metres (328 feet) apart along the hard shoulder.

The arrow directs you to the nearest phone on your side of the carriageway. Walk to the telephone, keeping on the inside of the hard shoulder.

Never   cross the carriageway or an exit or entry slip road to reach a phone or for any other purpose.

Using the emergency phone The telephone connects you to police control, who will put you through to a breakdown service. Always face the traffic when you speak on the telephone.

You'll be asked for

- the number on the telephone, which gives your precise location

- details of your vehicle and your membership details, if you belong to one of the motoring organisations

- details of the fault.

If you're a vulnerable motorcyclist such as a woman travelling alone, make this clear to the operator.

You'll also be told approximately how long you'll have to wait.

Mobile phones If you are unable to use an emergency telephone, use a mobile phone if you have one. However, before you call, make sure that you can give the police precise details of your location. Marker posts on the side of the hard shoulder identify your location and you should provide these details when you call.

Waiting for the emergency services

Many motorway deaths are caused by vehicles driving into people on the hard shoulder. For this reason wait on the bank near your vehicle, so you can see the emergency services arriving.

To rejoin the motorway

Don't pull straight out onto the carriageway. Use the hard shoulder as an acceleration lane to build up speed before joining the left-hand lane when there's a gap.

Roadworks

Accidents can often happen at roadworks when drivers fail to observe simple rules of safety. So

- reduce speed in good time when warned by the advance warning signs or flashing signals
- get into the lane indicated for use by your vehicle in good time
- obey all speed limits
- keep the correct separation distance from the vehicle ahead
- avoid sharp braking and sudden changes of direction
- don't change lanes when signs tell you to stay in your lane
- don't let your concentration wander
- don't speed up until you're clear of the roadworks.

Contraflow systems

These are temporary systems where traffic travelling in opposite directions shares the same carriageway.

They allow traffic to keep moving during repairs or alterations on the other carriageway.

The lanes are often narrower than normal lanes. Red and white marker posts separate traffic travelling in opposite directions and fluorescent or reflective bright green/yellow studs often replace normal ones.

Note While contraflow systems are usually found on motorways, they may also be used on other roads carrying fast-moving traffic.

Watch out for

- lane change signs
- vehicles broken down ahead. There's often no hard shoulder
- vehicles braking ahead – **keep your distance.**

Mobile roadworks

Minor maintenance work may sometimes be carried out without the need for major lane closures. Slow moving or stationary works vehicles, with a large arrow on the back of the vehicle, are used to divert traffic to the right or left as appropriate.

There are no cones or other delineators when these vehicles are being used.

The weather in the British Isles is varied and uncertain. You can expect to encounter virtually all weather conditions at some time.

The weather presents particular hazards for the motorcyclist. You need to think about how you're going to

- protect yourself from the elements
- adapt your riding to suit the conditions.

As you gain experience you'll find that it pays to be prepared for the worst kind of weather for the time of year. You'll also find that there are some weather conditions when it's better not to ride at all.

The topics covered

- your motorcycle
- weather and vision
- riding on wet roads
- riding in fog
- riding in cold weather
- riding in windy weather
- riding in sunshine and hot weather.

Your motorcycle

Whatever the weather, make sure your motorcycle is in good condition and regularly checked and serviced. Contending with the elements can be difficult but having to contend with a poorly performing motorcycle at the same time is an extra difficulty you should avoid.

Tyres

Be prepared: don't wait until the bad weather before checking your tyres.

Check for

- tread depth
- pressure
- objects stuck in the tyre
- cuts or damage.

Your safety could depend on a few millimetres of rubber which should have been there.

Incorrect tyre pressures can cause

- loss of stability
- reduced grip
- increased wear.

Brakes

Keep your brakes in good condition. Wet weather will increase your stopping distance even with perfect brakes.

Electrics

Motorcycle electrical systems are exposed to the elements. Damp or wet affecting your ignition systems can cause

- starting problems
- the engine to misfire. A misfiring engine will cause loss of power and may stop running altogether.

Keep your battery in good condition. In cold weather an electric starter places big demands on the battery.

Lights

Always keep your lights and indicators clean and check for faulty bulbs. Dirty lights can seriously reduce

- how far you can see
- how well other people can see you and your signals.

Weather and vision

The biggest single danger to any rider is being unable to see properly. You won't be able to make the right decisions if you can't see the road clearly.

Rain

Heavy rain on your visor or goggles can affect your view of the road. If you can't see clearly, stop and demist your visor or goggles. It's a good idea to carry a cloth with you especially for this purpose.

If you wear glasses it may be that they too have misted over. Don't be tempted to ride without your glasses if you need them to bring your eyesight up to the legal requirement.

Some modern helmets have air vents to help prevent fogging up and anti-fog products are also available.

Keeping dry If you allow yourself to get wet you'll also get cold. Being cold and wet can seriously reduce your ability to concentrate.

Proper motorcycle clothing is available which will keep you dry in the heaviest downpour. Good motorcycle clothing is a must if you intend to ride in bad weather.

Fog

When riding in fog you may have the combined problems of

- fogging up on the inside of visors or goggles, and

- misting over on the outside of visors or goggles.

Water droplets can form evenly across the outside of your visor or goggles. This can be difficult to detect since it appears the loss of vision is being caused by the density of the fog rather than this mist of water droplets. Frequently wipe your visor or goggles to prevent this mist obscuring your view of the road.

In freezing fog the mist build up can quickly freeze over. Once frozen you will have to stop and de-ice your visor or goggles to restore a clear view.

Being seen Making yourself visible to other road users is important at all times. In the rain and fog it's especially so, because of the reduction in visibility.

Wear bright, high visibility clothing and keep your headlamp on dipped beam.

DSA MOTORCYCLE RIDING

Riding on wet roads

Wet roads reduce tyre grip. Give yourself plenty of time and room for slowing down and stopping. Keep well back from other vehicles.

On a wet road, you should allow at least double the braking distance for a dry road.

After a spell of dry weather, rain on the road can make the surface even more slippery. Take extra care, especially when cornering.

Be aware that different road surfaces might affect the grip of your tyres.

Brakes

As well as reducing tyre grip water can also reduce the effectiveness of your brakes. You should allow for this and keep your speed down.

A wet road means

- less efficient braking
- a longer distance to stop
- a greater risk of skidding.

If the surface is good but wet, you should

- aim to brake when the machine is in its most stable position, that is, upright and moving straight ahead
- apply the front brake slightly before the rear. Spread the braking effort evenly between the front and rear brakes.

Motorcyclists need to be aware of slippery surfaces caused by rain on

- metal drain covers
- leaves
- muddy roads
- fuel spillages. This may appear as a rainbow coloured film on the road surface
- painted road markings.

These surfaces need extra care when cornering or braking.

layer of water

displaced water

Surface water

When the rain is very heavy or if the road has poor drainage you'll have to deal with surface water.

If you ride too fast through surface water your tyres might not be able to displace water quickly enough. A thin film of water can then build up between the tyre and the road so that the tyre loses contact with the road and all grip is lost. The effect is called 'aquaplaning'. High speed and worn tyres increase the risk of aquaplaning.

To avoid aquaplaning

* keep your speed down
* avoid riding through water pooling on the road suface – if you can do so safely.

If you feel your motorcycle start to aquaplane ease off the throttle. Don't brake or turn the steering until grip is restored.

Try not to splash pedestrians by riding through pools of water close to the kerb.

Floods

Before you ride through flood water stop and assess how deep the water is. Sometimes roads that flood regularly have depth gauges. You can check the depth on these.

If the water seems too deep turn back and go around the flood by another route. It may take a little longer but it's better than becoming stranded in the flood.

If the water is not too deep, ride through slowly and

* keep in a low gear
* keep your engine running fast enough to prevent water entering the exhaust
* try to ride where the water is most shallow. Due to camber on roads this is likely to be in the crown of the road. Watch for oncoming vehicles who may be doing the same thing
* test your brakes when you're out of the water.

Crossing a ford

Where a ford crosses a road the road surface is also a stream bed. It may

- be very uneven with loose stones
- have a slippery coating over many of the surfaces
- have a strong current.

This can all make riding through a ford a very hazardous activity.

The depth of water at fords varies with the weather and is usually greater in winter.

There may be a depth gauge.

If the water is not too deep for your motorcycle, cross using the same technique as you would for a flood. Remember to test your brakes after you cross. There might be a notice reminding you to do so.

Don't

Don't try to displace the water by 'charging' at the flood or ford.

- Your motorcycle may stall.
- You could lose control resulting in
  - falling off
  - injury to yourself, your passenger or another road user
  - damage to property.
- You could end up blocking the road.

Riding in fog

Fog is one of the most dangerous weather conditions.

An accident involving one vehicle can quickly involve many others, especially if they're travelling too close to one another.

Motorway pile-ups in fog have sometimes involved dozens of vehicles.

All too often, there's a loss of life or serious injury, which could so easily be prevented.

Observe the obvious

It doesn't need a sign to tell you it's foggy if you can only see a short distance ahead!

Remember

If the fog is very thick and you can see the rear lights of the vehicle ahead, then

You're probably too close to stop in an emergency.

Avoid riding in fog

Take alternative transport or postpone your journey, if at all possible.

If you must make the journey, give yourself time to prepare, check all lights, clean your visor or goggles, and so on. Allow more time for the journey.

Fog patches

The density of fog varies. Sometimes the fog is patchy. One moment it can be fairly clear, the next extremely dense. Avoid the temptation to speed up between the patches.

Use of lights in fog

In daylight   You must use your dipped headlight when visibility is seriously reduced:

- it'll be seen from a much greater distance than sidelights
- it won't dazzle other road users or pedestrians in the daytime.

High-intensity rear fog lights   If your motorcycle has high-intensity rear fog lights, use them only in fog when visibility is less than 100 metres (328 feet).

You must switch them off when visibility improves – it is the law. Using them at other times, such as in the rain, can dazzle following drivers.

Don't   use main beam when you're in fog

- the fog reflects the light and can dazzle you, reducing your view even further
- you can dazzle other drivers.

Adjust your lights   Change your lighting with the conditions.

For example, when you're queuing in traffic and the driver behind has already seen you, it can be helpful to switch off your rear fog lights temporarily to avoid dazzle.

When riding in fog

Poor visibility is frustrating and puts a strain on the eyes. Your ability to anticipate is dangerously restricted.

It's also much more difficult to judge distances and speed in fog when outlines become confusing. You can easily become disoriented – especially on an unfamiliar road.

If you find yourself in fog

- slow down so that you can stop within your range of vision
- use your dipped headlight
- keep your visor or goggles clear
- keep your distance from the vehicle in front
- use your rear fog lamp (if fitted) when visibility falls below 100 metres (about 330 feet).

Positioning   Try to keep a central position between lane lines or studs.

Don't mix up lane lines and centre lines.

Riding too close to the centre could mean you're dangerously near someone coming the other way doing the same thing.

Riding on the centre line as a means of finding your way is extremely dangerous.

Don't ride in the gutter either as parked vehicles, cyclists and pedestrians could appear suddenly.

Following another vehicle in fog   Slow down and leave plenty of room for stopping.

There may be something ahead which you cannot possibly see until you're close to it.

If the vehicle ahead has to stop suddenly, you must have ample time to react and brake.

You may not see or recognise that the vehicle ahead is braking, or has stopped, as soon as you would in clear weather.

You need to be able to brake safely, so remember the road surface is often slippery in fog.

Overtaking   Overtaking in fog can be particularly dangerous. Never begin to overtake unless you can clearly see that it's safe to do so. There won't be many such opportunities when riding in mist or fog. You could well find that visibility ahead is much worse than you thought, and you won't be able to see oncoming traffic soon enough.

Junctions in fog Dealing with junctions in fog needs particular care, especially when turning right. Traffic will generally be moving more slowly and may be difficult to hear.

Do

- listen for approaching traffic
- start indicating as early as you can
- make the greatest possible use of your lights. If you keep your foot on the brake pedal while you're stopped, your brake lights will give drivers behind an extra warning
- use the horn if you feel it will help.

Don't turn until you're absolutely sure it's safe.

Road markings Dipped headlights will pick out reflective studs, but it's not so easy to recognise other road markings when driving in fog. Explanations of the different coloured studs are given in Part seven, under 'Road markings'.

Parking in fog

Never park on a road in the fog if you can avoid it. Find an off-street parking place.

However, if it is unavoidable, always leave your parking lights on.

Breaking down

If you break down, get your motorcycle off the road if you possibly can.

Inform the police, and make arrangements to remove it as soon as possible if it creates an obstruction.

Never leave it without warning lights of some kind or on the wrong side of the road.

Riding in cold weather

If you get cold when riding

- your concentration will suffer
- your ability to control your machine will be affected
- your enjoyment of motorcycling will be lessened.

Keeping warm can be a problem. There is motorcycle clothing available which will keep you warm in very low temperatures. This clothing isn't cheap, but it's essential if you want to ride in cold weather.

The cold will probably affect your hands and feet first. Don't continue if you lose feeling in your fingers or toes. Stop now and then to warm up.

Snow and ice

It's better not to ride at all in conditions of snow and ice. If you must travel in these conditions keep to the main roads. These are more likely to be clear and well gritted.

When riding on snow or ice your tyres have reduced grip on the road. Keep your speed down and take great care when

- accelerating
- braking
- cornering.

Snow   In falling snow, use your dipped headlight and keep your visor or goggles clear. Snow will quickly cover road signs and markings. Be aware of the danger this creates.

Snow can also build up over your headlight and front indicators as you ride. This will quickly reduce their effectiveness. If this happens stop frequently to clear the snow away.

Ice Overnight freezing usually results in an icy surface, especially on less used roads. Look for signs of frost on verges, etc.

It's even more dangerous when the roads are just beginning to freeze or thaw. The combination of water and ice adds up to an extremely slippery surface.

You need to watch for areas where ice may linger after it's cleared elsewhere. This may be

* areas of shade caused by features such as trees, hedges, and buildings
* exposed roads where wind chill keeps the ground temperature low
* low lying areas where cold air gathers
* shaded hills and slopes

Other road users may not appreciate how severely the conditions are affecting you. If someone is following too closely, pull over and let them go past.

Black ice Black ice is very dangerous. It forms when droplets of water freeze on a normally good skid resistant surface. Black ice is so dangerous because it's almost invisible.

In wintry conditions, if the road looks wet but you can't hear tyre noise as you would on a wet road, suspect black ice.

Riding in windy weather

A strong gust of wind from one side can suddenly blow you off course. You're likely to be affected by these crosswinds

- as you pass gateways or gaps in hedges
- as you pass gaps in buildings
- as you pass high-sided vehicles
- on exposed roads.

When it's windy keep your speed down so that you can remain in control. Look ahead and anticipate places where crosswinds may affect you.

Crosswinds can affect other road users too. These include

- cyclists
- high-sided vehicles
- vehicles towing trailers or caravans.

DSA MOTORCYCLE RIDING

Riding in sunshine and hot weather

Motorcycling is probably at its best during warm, dry weather.

Clear visor/goggles

There are generally more flies and insects about in hot weather, and they can soon cause a dirty and smeary visor or goggles. This can

- reduce your view of the road, especially at night
- worsen the effects of glare.

Always keep your visor or goggles clean and free from smears (see Part four, under 'Cleaning your visor or goggles').

Dust and dirt can cause tiny scratches on visors and goggles. These scratches build up over time. Replace your visor or goggles if they become heavily scratched.

Clothing

Never be tempted to ride without wearing protective clothing, even on the hottest days. You could be horribly injured from even the most minor accident.

Never ride
- **In shorts or trainers**
- **Bare-armed**

Always wear full protective clothing.

Glare

Constant sun in your eyes can be exhausting on a long journey and may well affect your concentration.

Even if you don't feel the need, the correct sunglasses can reduce the glare and keep your eyes efficient for longer.

This is especially important if you're riding abroad, where conditions are hotter and the sunlight brighter than you may be used to.

If the roads are wet, reflected glare seriously reduces your ability to see. Reduce speed and take extra care.

Low-angle sun   Glare can be worse in the winter when the sun is low in the sky. Wearing sunglasses or using an approved tinted visor can help to reduce the glare. If you're affected, slow down so that you can stop within the distance you can see. Avoid looking directly into the sun.

Remember

you must not wear tinted glasses, visors or goggles

- in the dark
- during conditions of poor visibility.

Road surface

During a long hot, dry spell the road surface will become coated with rubber, particularly at

- junctions
- bends
- roundabouts.

When it rains after such a dry spell the road will be unusually slippery. Look out for shiny surfaces.

Loose chippings Many highway authorities replace the granite chipping road surfaces during the summer. While this work is being carried out you may have to ride on temporary road surfaces. These can be very rough and watch for humps at the beginning and end of the temporary surface:

- take extra care
- observe the special warning speed limits
- keep well back from the vehicle in front.

When a road has been resurfaced with chippings it has a very loose surface for several days. Loose chippings will reduce your tyres' grip on the road. When riding on loose chippings, take care when

- accelerating
- braking
- cornering.

Watch for the warning signs and reduced speed limits.

Flying stone chips can cause

- expensive damage to your vehicle
- eye injury if you ride without wearing goggles or with your visor raised
- serious injury to pedestrians and other road users.

Soft tarmac During long periods of hot weather, many tarmac road surfaces become extremely soft. Take care braking and cornering. Melted tar can reduce tyre grip and lead to skidding.

Riding at night is another aspect of motorcycling which demands special techniques and precautions. The problems of riding at night vary with the type of road and the amount of traffic, but this part deals with the most important aspects.

The topics covered

- seeing at night
- lights
- being seen
- built-up areas
- overtaking or following at night
- parking at night
- meeting other vehicles.

Seeing at night

You should have your eyesight checked regularly.

Ask yourself, 'Can I really see as well as I would like?'

If you can't see so well at night, it might be your eyes that are to blame; night riding may be highlighting the need for an eyesight check.

How far can you see?

Test yourself in a suitable place.

Pick an object within the range of your lights and see if you can stop by the time you reach it.

You'll be surprised how difficult this is with dipped lights on an unlit road, and shows that you should take a good look before you dip your lights.

Adjusting to darkness

Give your eyes a minute or two to adjust to the darkness, particularly when you're coming out of a brightly lit area or building.

Remember this when you leave a motorway service area after a rest or refuelling stop.

To help you see at night you should keep your goggles or visor clean. Scratches on either can cause dazzle from approaching traffic. If your goggles or visor become scratched you should replace them.

If you're riding in the dark don't wear

- sunglasses
- tinted goggles
- a tinted visor.

Lights

To help other road users to see you, ride with your headlight on dipped beam at **all times** – even in good daylight.

At night, your vehicle lights are the most important source of information for both you and for other road users.

- Keep your lights clean.
- Check all your lights before any journey.
- Fix any lighting fault immediately, for your own safety, and the safety of others. Carry spare bulbs.
- Practise operating the light switches so that you can find them easily in the dark.
- Remember that extra weight of a pillion passenger or a load could cause your headlight to aim higher than normal. This could cause
  - dazzle to other road users
  - reduced effectiveness of your headlight

  Adjust your headlight to deal with this.

Using dipped beam

You must use a dipped headlight

- at night when street lighting is poor (street lights more than 185 metres (600 feet) apart)
- in poor visibility
- at night on all other roads including motorways.

Using main beam

Use your headlight on main beam in any conditions where the main beam will help you to see without dazzling other road users.

When your headlight is on main beam the blue main beam warning lamp will glow.

Dipping your headlight Dip your main beam

- in the face of oncoming traffic
- when approaching traffic from behind.

Don't dazzle other road users – you could cause an accident.

When you dip your headlight

- you'll see less of the road ahead
- slow down so that you can stop within the distance you can see.

 MOTORCYCLE RIDING

Being seen

At night it's more difficult for other road users to see you in good time. In congested urban areas a single motorcycle headlight can get lost in the background of distracting lights.

Be aware of the difficulty other road users might have and

- ride with dipped beam, unless you need to use the full beam
- wear reflective clothing. Fluorescent clothing won't show in the dark
- keep your lamps clean and working correctly
- keep your reflective number plate clean.

Built-up areas

Always use dipped beam in built-up areas at night. It helps others to see you!

In areas where street lights cause patches of shadow, watch out for pedestrians, especially those in dark clothes, who can be difficult to see.

Remember

- be on the alert for pedestrians
- approach pedestrian crossings at a speed at which you can stop safely if necessary
- watch for cyclists and joggers.

Noise at night

Keep all noise to a minimum and try not to disturb residents who may be asleep:

- don't rev your engine unnecessarily
- take extra care setting or disarming any anti-theft alarm on your motorcycle.

Using the horn at night   You must not use your horn between 11.30 pm and 7 am in a built-up area (except to avoid danger from a moving vehicle).

If you need to warn other road users of your presence at night, flash your headlight.

Overtaking or following at night

You'll need to take extra care before attempting to overtake at night. It's more difficult because you can see less.

Only overtake if you can see that the road ahead will remain clear until after you have finished the manoeuvre.

Don't overtake if there's a chance you are approaching

- a road junction
- a bend
- the brow of a bridge or hill, except on a dual carriageway
- a pedestrian crossing
- double white lines ahead

or if there's likely to be

- a vehicle overtaking or turning right
- any other potential hazard.

Stay clear and dip

Make sure you don't get too close to the vehicle ahead, and always dip your headlight so you don't cause dazzle.

Your light beam should fall short of the rear of the vehicle in front.

Remember your separation distance.

On a dual carriageway or motorway where it's possible to overtake, don't use full beam in the face of oncoming drivers.

If you're being overtaken

Dip your headlight as soon as the vehicle passes you.

Parking at night

Cars, light goods vehicles (1525 kg or less unladen) and motorcycles can park without lights on roads with a speed limit of 30 mph or less. They must comply with any parking restrictions, and not park within 10 metres (32 feet) of a junction.

They must also be parked parallel to, and close to, the side of the road or in a designated parking place and facing in the direction of the traffic flow.

Always

Switch your headlight off when you stop, even for a short while.

It's an offence to leave it on when parked. The fixed glare can be very dazzling, especially if, for any reason, you've parked on the offside of the road facing oncoming traffic.

Never

- leave your motorcycle on any other road without using the parking lights unless a sign indicates that lights are not required; it's better to get it off the road altogether
- leave your motorcycle standing on the right-hand side of the road, except in a one-way street.

Meeting other vehicles

Another vehicle's lights can tell you which direction they're heading and can give you an idea of their speed. Oncoming lights should raise a number of questions in your mind, such as

- how far away is the vehicle and how fast is it moving?
- should I slow down while we pass each other?
- how soon should I dip my headlight?
- how far ahead can I see before I dip?
- before I dip, is there anything on my side of the road
  - that I might endanger?
  - that might endanger me?

  for example, a stationary vehicle, a cyclist, a pedestrian, or an unlit obstacle.

Headlight on full beam

When your headlight is on full beam

- dip early enough to avoid dazzling oncoming drivers, but not too early
- check the left-hand verge before you dip.

When you're dazzled

If the headlights of oncoming vehicles dazzle you, slow down and, if necessary, stop.

Don't look directly at oncoming headlights.

Don't retaliate by leaving your headlight on full beam and dazzling the oncoming driver.

On a left-hand bend

Dip earlier.

Your headlight will cut straight across the eyes of anyone coming toward you.

On a right-hand bend this might not happen, or it won't happen so soon.

Riding with a passenger or a load can call for adjustments to your machine as well as your riding.

You must not carry a pillion passenger or pull a trailer unless you have a full motorcycle licence. However, all riders are allowed to carry loads and there are various methods available, including

- panniers
- top box
- tank bag
- luggage rack.

In addition, a sidecar outfit can be fitted to suitable machines. This provides additional carrying capacity for passengers and loads. This part covers the problems and techniques of carrying passengers and loads.

The topics covered

- carrying a passenger
- carrying a load
- sidecar outfits
- towing a trailer.

Carrying a passenger

Legal requirements

Before you can carry a passenger you must comply with the law.

You're allowed to carry a pillion passenger only if

- you've passed your practical motorcycle test
- you hold a full motorcycle licence for the category of machine you're riding.

To carry a passenger your motorcycle should have

- rear footrests
- a proper passenger seat.

Motorcycle adjustments

To cope with the extra load of a pillion passenger you should

- inflate the tyres according to the maker's instructions
- adjust the pre-load on the rear shock absorbers to allow for the extra weight. See your owner's handbook for details
- adjust the headlamp aim, if necessary.

Passengers

If your passenger has never ridden pillion before, or you doubt their experience, instruct them to

- sit astride the machine facing forwards
- wear an approved motorcycle helmet, properly fastened
- keep both feet on the passenger footrests until dismounting
- keep a light but firm hold on your waist or the passenger grab handle (if fitted)
- lean with you while going around bends or corners.

Instruct your passenger not to

- look behind or signal for you
- lean to the side to see ahead. This might affect your balance and stability.

Passenger's clothing   Your passenger's clothing should be

- weatherproof and protective
- bright and, if riding at night, reflective.

Don't allow your passenger to wear a scarf or belt loosely fastened. These can get tangled in the wheel or drive chain and cause serious injury.

Riding techniques

Until you get used to carrying a passenger, ride with extra care. The passenger will affect

- your balance, especially at low speeds
- your ability to stop. The extra weight may increase your stopping distance. Allow a bigger gap when following another vehicle
- your acceleration. You'll be slower getting moving so allow more room when emerging at junctions.

Don't

- carry children on a motorcycle unless they can safely use the footrests and handholds
- ask your passenger to look behind or signal for you
- accept any road or traffic information from your passenger without verifying it.

Carrying a load

To carry a load on a motorcycle you can use

- panniers
- top box
- tank bag
- luggage rack.

Panniers

There are two types of panniers available:

- rigidly fixed
- throw-over saddlebag.

Whichever type you use, always make sure that you load them evenly. Uneven loading can lead to loss of stability.

Top box

A top box is fastened onto a rack behind the seat. It's easy and quick to use but has its limitations. The weight is carried high up and at the very back of the machine. Don't carry heavy loads in a top box because this can

- reduce stability
- cause low-speed wobble
- cause high-speed weave.

Tank bag

A tank bag is fastened on top of the fuel tank (or dummy tank) and can carry large loads. Take care that the tank bag doesn't interfere with your ability to steer.

Luggage rack

Make sure that any items strapped onto the luggage rack are securely fastened. A loose load could become tangled in the rear wheel and cause an accident.

Adjusting your motorcycle

Make any necessary adjustments to the

- suspension
- tyres
- lights.

When riding with a load give yourself the chance to get used to the extra weight. If the load is unevenly distributed and your machine is unbalanced stop and rearrange the load.

Sidecar outfits

If you want to fit a sidecar you should

* ask your dealer if your machine is suitable
* make sure that, after fitting, the sidecar is fixed correctly to the mounting points
* in the UK, sidecars should be fitted only on the left-hand side of the machine if the machine was registered on or after 1 August 1981.

Aligning the sidecar

Make sure that the bike and sidecar are correctly aligned. If they aren't the outfit will be difficult to control and probably dangerous.

Riding techniques

You must adapt your riding technique when riding a bike with a sidecar. Keep your speed down until you've become used to the outfit.

On bends and when turning, the sidecar outfit must be steered because you can't lean the machine over. This requires a deliberate push or pull on the handlebar.

On left-hand bends the sidecar wheel will tend to lift as the weight is thrown outwards. This calls for special care and control.

Braking

Unless a brake is fitted to the sidecar wheel the outfit will tend to pull to the right under heavy braking.

The extra weight of the sidecar may increase the overall stopping distance.

Sidecar outfits need special care on bends.

Towing a trailer

You can only tow a trailer behind your motorcycle if

- you have a full motorcycle licence
- your machine has an engine capacity exceeding 125 cc
- the trailer doesn't exceed 1 metre (just over 3 feet) in width
- the distance between the rear axle of the motorcycle and the rear of the trailer is less than 2.5 metres (about 8 feet)
- the motorcycle is clearly marked with its kerbside weight
- the trailer is clearly marked with its unladen weight
- the laden weight of the trailer doesn't exceed 150 kg or two thirds of the kerbside weight of the motorcycle, whichever is less.

You can't tow

- more than one trailer
- a trailer carrying a passenger.

When you tow a trailer remember that

- you must obey the speed limit restrictions which apply for all vehicles towing trailers
- your stopping distance may be increased
- any load in the trailer must be secure
- the trailer must be fitted to the machine correctly.

Don't forget it's there!

A motorcycle needs routine attention and maintenance to keep it in a roadworthy condition. Learning how to carry out routine maintenance yourself will save you time and money.

Many routine maintenance jobs are straightforward and explained in the owner's handbook. More difficult tasks may need to be referred to your dealer.

Rider training courses may include some mechanical instructions and advice on maintenance.

The topics covered

- regular checks
- engine
- suspension and steering
- controls
- electrical systems.

Regular checks

You should check the following items on a regular basis:

Engine

- fuel
- oil.
  - engine
  - gearbox
  - final drive
- coolant (liquid cooled engines)
- air filter.

Suspension and steering

- suspension
- steering head bearings
- wheels
- tyres.

Controls

- brakes
- clutch
- throttle.

Electrical systems

- battery
- lights
- horn
- indicators.

Brake, clutch, throttle

Battery electrolyte

Shock absorbers

Rear lamp and indicators

Tyres and wheels

Brakes

Drive chain

Engine and gearbox oil

Brake fluid

Front lamps and indicator

Steering head bearings

Horn

Forks

Brakes

Tyres and wheels

Engine

A properly maintained engine will

- start more easily
- use less fuel
- be more reliable
- give optimum performance
- have lower exhaust emissions.

Items which will affect the engine performance include

- spark plugs
- ignition settings
- air filter
- carburettor settings
- valve clearances.

If you aren't confident in your ability to maintain your engine, entrust the work to your dealer.

Fuel

Many modern motorcycles are fitted with fuel gauges and low fuel level warning lamps which flash when petrol levels are low.

If your motorcycle doesn't have a fuel gauge you'll have to remove the filler cap to check how much fuel you have.

Some motorcycles have a reserve supply of petrol which is accessed by setting the petrol tap to a reserve position (see Part five, under 'Typical position of controls'). The amount of petrol held in this reserve varies with makes and models but typically may be enough to ride 20 – 30 miles.

When the main tank becomes empty the engine will lose power, and it may cough or even cut out altogether. The petrol tap needs to be moved into the reserve position and there may be a slight lag before the fuel reaches the engine. This could be hazardous in certain circumstances, and it is advisable to refuel before the reserve level is reached.

For motorcycles that don't have a fuel gauge it's a good idea to reset the trip meter when you refuel. You can use the mileage to indicate when you need to refuel again.

Motorcycle engines Two types of petrol engines are fitted to motorcycles:

- two-stroke engines
- four-stroke engines.

If you don't know which type of engine is fitted to your motorcycle, check the owner's manual or ask your dealer.

Two-stroke engines The two-stroke engine runs on a combined petrol/oil mixture. A special two-stroke oil needs to be combined with the petrol in a ratio determined by the manufacturer. This may be 20:1, for example. Two-stroke oil is combined with the petrol by either

- directly adding the oil to the petrol when refuelling
- adding two-stroke oil to a special oil tank. The oil is then automatically mixed with the petrol as it is fed into the engine.

When refuelling a motorcycle with a two-stroke engine you must remember to add/check two-stroke oil.

Four-stroke engine It's important that you use the correct grade of petrol for your engine. Most modern four-stroke motorcycle engines run on unleaded fuel but older models may require lead replacement petrol. Check with your dealer/manufacturer if you aren't sure, or check with an oil company's technical department if you are running an older motorcycle.

Catalytic converter Leaded or lead replacement fuel must not be used on a motorcycle fitted with a catalytic converter. Even one tankful can permanently damage the system.

Oil

Oil is necessary to lubricate your engine. You need to keep the oil at the level recommended by the vehicle manufacturer.

Check regularly and top up the oil when necessary, especially before a long journey.

How to check the oil level Your motorcycle will have either

• a dipstick

• a sightglass

to tell you the amount of oil in the engine. See the owner's handbook.

Checking the oil while the engine is cold will give a more accurate result:

• ensure the vehicle is on a level area and parked on the centre stand

• locate either the dipstick or sightglass on your motorcycle.

Motorcycles with a sightglass You may need a cloth to wipe the sightglass clean. The oil level should be between the 'max' and 'min' marks. If the level is too low top it up to the correct level using the manufacturer's recommended grade of oil.

Motorcycles with a dipstick Remove the dipstick and wipe it clean. Return it fully into the dipstick opening and then remove it again and look to see the oil level. If the level is too low, top it up to the correct level using the manufacturer's recommended grade of oil.

Oil changes Observe the manufacturer's recommendations. If a large number of short journeys are involved, change the oil at more frequent intervals, especially in dusty conditions. Remember to have the oil filter changed at the same time.

DSA MOTORCYCLE RIDING

Warning

Oil is toxic and can cause skin problems. Wash it off your hands immediately.

Keep containers storing oil out of reach of children.

Oil use   The amount of oil an engine will use depends on

- the type of engine
- the amount of wear
- how you ride.

Don't

- run the engine when the oil level is below the minimum mark
- add so much oil that the level rises above the maximum mark. You'll create excess pressure that could damage the engine seals and gaskets, and cause oil leaks.

Warning light   If the oil pressure warning light on your instrument panel comes on when you're riding, stop as soon as you can and check the oil level.

Lubricating oils – engine   The oil in your engine has to perform several tasks at high pressures and temperatures up to 300° C. It helps to

- resist wear on the moving surfaces
- combat the corrosive acids formed as the hydrocarbons in the fuels are burnt in the engine
- keep the engine cool.

It also has to withstand gradual contamination from both fuel and dirt.

Make sure you always use the lubricants recommended in the handbook.

Lubricating oils – gearbox   Most motorcycles use the engine oil to lubricate the gearbox. A few, however, have a separate lubricating oil supply for the gearbox.

This oil is especially formulated for use in the gearbox and you should always follow the instructions in the vehicle handbook.

It's not necessary to drain the gearbox in most cases, but the level should be checked at service intervals.

Lubricating oils – shaft final drive

Motorcycles with a shaft final drive have a separate supply held in the final drive housing on the rear wheel hub.

There's a filler/level hole on the housing. Remember to have the motorcycle upright when checking the final drive oil level.

It's important that the correct hypoid-type EP (extreme pressure) oil specified in the vehicle handbook is used.

You may have to squeeze the top-up oil using a plastic bottle and tube.

Lubricating oils – chain final drive   Final drive chains wear and require frequent lubrication and adjustment. Special motorcycle chain lubricants are available for this purpose. Allowing your drive chain to run dry will greatly increase the rate of wear.

The drive chain needs to be adjusted until the free play is as specified in the handbook.

When you've adjusted the chain tension you need to check the rear wheel alignment. Marks by the chain adjusters may be provided to make this easy.

If the chain is worn or slack it can jump off the sprocket and lock the rear wheel.

Coolant

Many motorcycle engines are liquid cooled using a mixture of water and anti-freeze. The anti-freeze contains a corrosion inhibitor which reduces rust and prolongs the life of the system. In cold weather, maintain the recommended strength of anti-freeze. Have it checked annually.

You should frequently check the coolant level, particularly before a long trip, topping up with coolant as necessary. The need to top up often might indicate a leak or other fault in the cooling system. Have it checked by your garage/dealer.

Air filter

Replace the air filter at the intervals recommended by the manufacturer, or sooner if the vehicle is used in exceptionally dusty conditions.

Warning
- Never remove a radiator cap when the engine is hot.
- Never add cold water to an overheated engine.

Suspension and steering

There are several different types of
suspension fitted to motorcycles. These range
from simple systems with no adjustment to
sophisticated systems adjustable for

- preload
- compression
- rebound.

Check your shock absorbers for oil leaks. A
faulty oil seal will allow the damping oil to
leak out and this can

- make the motorcycle difficult to control
- increase your stopping distance.

There is also a danger that oil leaking from
the front forks or a faulty shock absorber
may find its way onto the wheel, tyre and
brake disc or drum.

Steering head bearings

Steering head bearings allow smooth steering
movement. The bearings need to be checked
for wear and correct adjustment. Badly
adjusted or worn steering head bearings can
make the motorcycle difficult to control and
may lead to

- weaving
- wobbling.

Steering movement

The handlebars should be free to move from
full left lock to full right lock without

- any control cables being stretched,
  trapped or pinched
- any snagging between moving and fixed
  parts.

Wheels

Motorcycles are fitted with

- spoked wheels
- alloy wheels
- pressed steel wheels (small-wheeled machines only).

Check that the wheels are running 'true'. Spin each wheel in turn and watch where it passes a suspension arm or mudguard stay. If the wheel is buckled this will show up.

Check spoked wheels for loose or broken spokes, and all wheels for cracks or visible damage.

Regularly check wheel nuts and bolts for tightness.

Have your wheels balanced regularly by an authorised dealer or tyre fitter.

Wheel alignment It is important for the rear wheel to be aligned precisely behind the front. When adjusting the drive chain or refitting the rear wheel it is possible to disturb the wheel alignment. Incorrectly aligned wheels can cause

- instability, especially when cornering
- increased tyre wear.

Many motorcycles have wheel alignment guides stamped onto the frame by the chain adjusters. See your owner's manual for details.

Tyres

Incorrectly inflated tyres can cause

- loss of stability
- reduced grip
- increased tyre wear.

Check your tyre pressure

- at least every two weeks
- when the tyres are cold.

The correct tyre pressure settings can be found in the owner's manual.

You might have to increase the tyre pressure

- when carrying a pillion passenger
- when carrying loads
- when riding at sustained high speeds.

In addition, check your tyres for

- tread depth and uneven tread wear
- cuts or splits
- small stones, glass or any other object stuck in the tyre
- grease or oil which could affect the tyre's grip.

If there's any sign that the tyres have been damaged they should be replaced.

Regulations   You must not use any tyre that has

- a cut longer than 25 mm or 10 per cent of the width of the tyre, whichever is the greater, and which is deep enough to reach the ply
- a lump, bulge or tear caused by the part failure of its structure
- any exposed ply or cord
- been recut.

Minimum tread   The base of any groove which showed in the original tread must be seen clearly.

The grooves on the tread pattern of all tyres must not be less than 1 mm deep, forming a continuous band at least three quarters of the breadth of the tread and all the way around.

The groove of the original tread must be visible all around the tyre.

Most tyres have tread wear indicators. These are small raised mouldings in the bottom of the tread grooves. These indicators are exposed when the tread is worn down to 1 mm. Some tyre manufacturers design the tyres so that wear indicators are exposed before the 1 mm minimum is reached. If you can see the wear indicators use a tread depth gauge to check how much tread remains.

DSA MOTORCYCLE RIDING

Motorcycles less than 50 cc If your motorcycle has an engine capacity of less than 50 cc the tread of the tyre may be less than 1 mm if the base of any groove which showed in the original tread can be seen clearly.

Punctures If your machine suddenly becomes unstable a puncture might be the cause. If this happens or a tyre bursts

- don't brake suddenly
- hold the handlebars firmly
- close the throttle to make the machine slow down
- try to keep a straight course
- stop gradually at the side of the road.

A punctured tyre should be properly repaired or replaced.

Replacing a tyre When replacing a tyre you should

- fit a tyre that is recommended by the manufacturer
- buy the correct type. Some machines require a different type of tyre on the front and back wheel
- make sure the tyre is fitted to rotate in the direction of the tyre rotation indicators.

Controls

Brakes

There are two types of braking system fitted to motorcycles

- mechanically operated
- hydraulically operated.

With use, various parts of the braking system will wear and need adjustment or replacement.

Mechanically operated   If your motorcycle has mechanically operated brake systems

- periodic adjustment is necessary to compensate for
  - the strain on brake cables causing them to stretch
  - wear of the brake pads or shoes
- keep the pivots and cables lubricated to maintain efficiency.

Hydraulically operated   If your motorcycle has hydraulic brakes, check

- brake fluid levels regularly
- couplings and joints for leaks
- flexible hoses for cuts or damage.

All braking systems   Brake pads and shoes gradually wear during use. Check and replace them as necessary.

Clutch

The clutch fitted may be

- cable operated
- hydraulically operated.

If your motorcycle has a cable operated clutch check

- free play on the lever is as specified in the owner's manual
- for fraying or chafing of the cable.

For motorcycles fitted with a hydraulically operated clutch you should check for

- fluid level
- couplings and joints for leaks
- flexible hoses for cuts or damage.

Cable lubrication

Keeping control cables lubricated will extend their life and prevent stiff operation caused by friction between the inner cable and the outer casing.

Throttle

The throttle may be a single or twin cable arrangement. Check the throttle

- for smooth operation
- that it closes fully when released.

Check the cable

- for fraying or chafing
- is not pulled when turning the steering from lock to lock.

Electrical systems

Battery

Some modern batteries are maintenance-free and sealed for life. The terminals should be secure, clean and greased.

When the battery is fitted with a filler cap or caps, check the level of the fluid. The plates in each cell should be covered. Top up with distilled water if necessary, but avoid overfilling.

Lights

Check the operation of the brake lights, front and rear lights, including indicators and hazard lights if fitted, each time you use the vehicle.

It's a good idea to carry a selection of spare bulbs and fuses. See your the owner's handbook for bulb/fuse replacement procedure.

Headlights must be properly adjusted to

- avoid dazzling other road users
- enable you to see the road ahead adequately.

All lights must

- be clean and in good working order
- show a steady light.

DSA MOTORCYCLE RIDING

The horn

Check the horn is working properly and sounding clearly. Take care not to alarm or annoy others when doing so..

Indicators, when fitted

* must be clearly visible and in good working order
* must flash between one and two times per second.

Accidents are always possible, even when riding with the greatest care.

This part looks at what you need to know if you are involved in an accident or come across the scene of an accident. If you're the first to arrive at an accident the safety of others might be in your hands. Knowledge and preparation can save lives.

You must also know when to inform the police and when to exchange details with other road users.

The topics covered

- at the scene of an accident
- first aid on the roads
- fire
- tunnels.

At the scene of an accident

If you're involved in an accident, you must stop.

If you're the first or among the first to arrive at the scene of an accident, remember

- further collisions can, and do, happen
- fire is a major hazard
- both the accident victims and helpers are in danger.

What to do

Warn other traffic Do this by

- switching on hazard warning lights (if fitted) or other lights
- displaying an advance warning triangle
- using any other means to warn other drivers.

Put out cigarettes or other fire hazards. Switch off your engine and warn others to do the same.

Call the emergency services if necessary.

Calling emergency services Give full details of the location and casualties. On a motorway, this could mean going to the next emergency telephone.

Mobile phones It can be very tempting to reach immediately for your mobile phone to call the emergency services.

Before you do, make sure you are able to tell them exactly where you are. This is particularly important on a motorway where imprecise details can cause great problems for the emergency services. Location details are given on marker posts located on the hard shoulder. Always check these before you make your call.

Dealing with those involved Move uninjured people away from the vehicles involved to a place of safety.

On a motorway, this should be away from the carriageway, hard shoulder or central reservation.

Don't move casualties trapped in vehicles unless they're in danger. Be prepared to give first aid as described later in this section.

Don't remove a motorcyclist's helmet unless it is essential to do so.

When an ambulance arrives, give the crew as many facts as you can (but not assumptions, diagnoses, etc).

Dangerous goods

If the accident involves a vehicle containing dangerous goods:

- switch off your engine and do not smoke
- keep well away from the vehicle
- call the emergency services and give the police or fire brigade as much information as possible about the labels and other markings. Do not use a mobile phone close to a vehicle carrying flammable loads
- beware of dangerous liquids, dust or vapours, no matter how small a concentration, or however minor the effects on you may seem.

Full details of hazard warning plates are given in *The Highway Code*.

Passing the scene of an accident

If you are not one of the first to arrive at the scene of an accident and enough people have already stopped to give assistance, you should continue past carefully and not be distracted by the accident.

If the accident is on the other side of a dual carriageway or motorway, don't slow down to look. You may cause another accident on your side of the road, or, at the very least, additional and unnecessary traffic congestion.

Remember

Always give way to emergency vehicles. Watch out for their blue flashing lights and listen for their warning sirens.

If you are involved in an accident

If there are injuries, ask someone to call an ambulance and the police

- Give whatever help you can. People who seem to be unhurt may be suffering from shock, and may in fact be unaware of their injuries.
- Ask yourself if you're hurt too. If in doubt, get a check-up at the hospital.

You must call the police

- if anyone's hurt
- if you've damaged someone else's property but can't find them to tell them.

Report the accident, in person, to the police as soon as possible, or in any case within 24 hours.

Witnesses Note any witnesses and try to make sure they don't go before you get their names and addresses.

Make a note of the numbers of any vehicles whose occupants might have witnessed the accident.

You'll need to exchange details and obtain

- other people's name, address and phone numbers

- the make and registration number(s) of the other vehicle(s) involved
- insurance details.

Find out vehicle owner's details too, if different.

Information Gather as much information as you can, such as

- damage and/or injuries caused
- weather conditions
- road conditions
- details of other vehicles. Record all information: the colour, condition, whether the lights were on, were they showing any indicator signals?
- what was said by you and other people
- identification numbers of police involved.

Take photographs If you have a camera it can be useful to take photographs at the scene.

Draw a map Show the situation before and after the accident, and give the distances

- between vehicles
- from road signs or junctions
- away from the kerb.

Note skid marks, where any witnesses were situated, street names and vehicle speeds and directions.

Statements If the police ask you for a statement, you don't have to make one straight away. It could be better to wait a while, even if you don't appear to be suffering from shock.

Write your statement later. Take care with the wording, and keep a copy.

First aid on the road

Any first aid given at the scene of an accident should only be looked on as a temporary measure until the emergency services arrive.

If you haven't any first aid training, the following points could be helpful.

Accident victims

It's essential that the following are given immediate priority if the casualty is unconscious and permanent injury is to be avoided:

A – the **airway** must be cleared and kept open.

B – **breathing** must be established and maintained.

C – blood **circulation** must be maintained and severe bleeding stopped.

Airway   Check for and relieve any obstruction to breathing. Unless you suspect head or neck injury, remove any obvious obstruction in the mouth (false teeth, chewing gum, etc.).

Breathing   Breathing should begin and colour improve.

If there's no improvement after the airway has been cleared

- tilt the head back very gently
- place a clean piece of material, such as a handkerchief, over the injured person's mouth
- pinch the casualty's nostrils together
- blow into the mouth until the chest rises. Take your mouth away and wait for the chest to fall

- repeat regularly once every four seconds until the casualty can breathe without help
- with babies and small children let your mouth surround their mouth and nose and breathe very gently
- don't give up. Never assume anyone is dead. Keep giving mouth to mouth resuscitation until the ambulance arrives.

Unconscious and breathing   Don't move a casualty unless there's further danger. Movement could add to a spinal/neck injury.

If breathing is difficult or stops, treat as recommended above.

It's vital to obtain professional assistance as soon as possible. Ensure someone dials 999.

Don't attempt to remove an injured motorcyclist's safety helmet unless it's essential – serious injury could result.

Circulation and bleeding Put firm pressure on the wound, without pressing on anything which might be caught in it. Use clean material if you can.

Secure a pad with a bandage or length of cloth.

If it's a limb that's bleeding but not broken, raise it to lessen the bleeding.

Reassurance Even apparently uninjured persons could be in shock; prompt treatment will help minimise it.

- Avoid unnecessary movement and reassure the casualty confidently.
- Keep the casualty comfortable and warm.
- Loosen any tight clothing.
- Try to make sure they're not left alone.
- Don't give casualties anything to eat or drink.
- If the casualty has to be moved for safety reasons, place him or her in the recovery position.
- Calm a hysterical person by talking to him or her in firm, quiet tones.

Burns Check the casualty for shock, and if possible, try to cool the burn.

Try to find a liquid that is clean, cold and non-toxic with which to douse it.

Do not try to remove anything which is stuck to the burn.

Carry a first aid kit

You might never need it, but it could save a life.

Learn first aid You can learn first aid from

- St John Ambulance Association and Brigade
- St Andrew's Ambulance Association
- British Red Cross Society.

Fire

Carrying a suitable fire extinguisher on your motorcycle may help you to put out a small fire. Remember, fire can spread with alarming speed and any fire should be treated with extreme caution.

- If the fire appears to be large **do not** try to tackle it; get well clear of the vehicle and leave it to the fire brigade
- **Do not** take any risks.

When using your motorcycle if you notice a strong smell of petrol, don't ignore it – investigate!

Tunnels

If you break down or have an accident in a tunnel

- switch on your hazard warning lights (if fitted)
- switch off the engine
- call for help from the nearest emergency point
- give first aid to any injured people, if you are able.

If your vehicle is on fire and you can ride it out of the tunnel, do so. If not

- pull over to the side, switch off the engine and put the machine on its stand
- attempt to put out the fire using either an extinguisher carried on your motorcycle or the one available in the tunnel
- call for help from the nearest emergency point
- move without delay to an emergency exit if you cannot put out the fire.

If the vehicle in front is on fire switch on your warning lights, then follow the above procedure, giving first aid to the injured if possible.

Transport is an essential part of modern life, but we cannot ignore its environmental consequences – local, regional and global.

There is increasing public concern for the protection of our environment, with the result that many manufacturers are devoting more time, effort and resources to the development of environmentally friendly vehicles, including motorcycles.

However, emissions from motorcycles already in use can also be reduced. Poor maintenance and inefficient riding techniques can lead to higher fuel consumption and more pollution.

The good news is that it isn't difficult to improve the environmental performance of your motorcycle. By taking a few simple steps you can do your bit and save yourself money into the bargain.

The topics covered

- the effects of pollution
- what *you* can do to help
- off-road activities.

The effects of pollution

Motor vehicles account for most of the movement of passengers and goods.

The increased number of vehicles on the roads damages the environment and results in

- changes to the landscape
- building deterioration
- bridge weakening
- changes to communities
- using up of natural resources
- disruption of wildlife
- air pollution.

Fuel combustion produces carbon dioxide, a major greenhouse gas, and transport accounts for about one fifth of the carbon dioxide we produce in this country.

Since pollution affects all of us it's in our own interests to take any steps we can to reduce the pollution we cause by fuel combustion.

What *you* can do to help

Use your motorcycle only when it is necessary:

- avoid using your motorcycle for very short journeys, especially when the engine is cold
- walk or use a pedal cycle for short journeys
- use public transport when you can
- if possible avoid using your motorcycle when air pollution is high. Information about air pollution is available from
  - the Air Pollution Information service
  - local newspapers
  - the radio
  - the Internet – www.aeat.co.uk/netcen/airqual/forecast/

Keep your motorcycle well maintained

- Make sure the engine is in tune. Badly tuned motorcycles use more fuel and emit more exhaust fumes. Most badly polluting motorcycles can be easily tuned by a garage, and at a low cost.

- Have your motorcycle serviced regularly. The cost of a service may well be less than the cost of running a badly maintained bike. Make sure your service includes an emissions check.

- Make sure your tyres are properly inflated. Under-inflated tyres increase fuel consumption and can affect handling.

Hypoid Gear Oil

SAE

Antifreeze

Use your motorcycle more efficiently:

- if the engine is cold when you start, push in the choke as soon as the engine will run smoothly without it

- switch the engine off if you are likely to be stuck in traffic for longer than two minutes, or if you are parked for any reason

- ride sensibly and always within the speed limit. Good riding habits save fuel

- use the appropriate gear and avoid over-revving in low gears

- wherever possible avoid rapid acceleration or heavy braking, as this leads to greater fuel consumption and more pollution

- slow down. Riding at 70 mph uses considerably more fuel to cover the same distance than riding at 50 mph

- check your fuel consumption regularly to make sure you're getting the most from your motorcycle.

Select for economy and low emissions:

- when buying a new motorcycle consider choosing a more fuel efficient model

- take used oil, old batteries and used tyres to a garage or local authority site for recycling or safe disposal. Don't pour used oil down the drain or into the ground. It's illegal, harmful to the environment and could lead to prosecution.

Off-road activities

If you take part in off-road activities,
remember:

*   avoid damaging fences, paths, grasslands, etc.
*   take care not to harm livestock or wildlife
*   respect the countryside in general
*   ride in a responsible manner at all times.

RECYCLE USED OIL

Taking your motorcycle abroad, or hiring one in the country you're visiting, gives you freedom and mobility.

You can

- plan your holiday around your interests or business commitments
- travel at your own pace
- stop when and where you like
- visit places of interest on the way
- discover the more remote places
- carry equipment such as camping gear.

This section summarises what you need to do to prepare for riding in Europe.

The topics covered

- travelling in Europe
- planning your journey
- your motorcycle
- motorcycling documents
- personal documents
- motoring regulations
- riding in Europe

Travelling in Europe

An extensive motorway network runs through most of Europe and there are regular ferry links from many UK ports.

You have more opportunity to choose routes which take you closer to your European destination.

The Channel Tunnel provides yet another link to continental Europe.

More countries

Many East European countries have now opened up their borders, so there's even more of Europe to explore.

Planning your journey

If you're planning to take your motorcycle abroad, the major motoring organisations can help you to organise and plan the details of your trip. They can

- save you time and money
- set up medical, travel and vehicle insurance
- provide equipment for minor repairs and breakdowns
- help you organise the correct documents for your motorcycle or trailer.

You can often make your trip much easier by using their facilities and experience.

Your route

Once you know which country you're going to visit, you can begin to plan your route.

Again, the motoring organisations can simplify this for you with

- computerised route guides
- summaries of motoring regulations
- details of tolls, etc.

They will recommend routes from continental ports or airports to specific destinations, using motorways for speed and convenience, or scenic routes for pleasure.

Your motorcycle

Before you travel abroad, have your motorcycle thoroughly checked and serviced. Checks to make include

- spare bulbs and fuses
- your toolkit; make sure all items are complete and in working order
- make sure you have your spare keys.

Lights

Your lights will need to be altered for riding on the right:

- deflectors are required in most countries. These prevent your dipped beam dazzling drivers approaching on the left
- yellow-tinted headlights are no longer required in most countries
- carry a set of replacement bulbs.

Emergency equipment

In many countries emergency equipment must be carried. Check with motoring organisations to find out what is required in the countries you will be visiting. This equipment may include

- emergency repair kits
- spares kit
- emergency warning triangle.

Precautions against breakdown

Dealing with breakdowns abroad can be especially time consuming and worrying without the help of one of the motoring organisations or breakdown services.

The best prevention is to have your motorcycle thoroughly serviced before you leave and to make regular checks on route.

You can also make sure you're prepared for minor breakdowns.

Motorcycling documents

You must have all the necessary documents before leaving. Again, the motoring organisations will be able to tell you what's required for each country.

Insurance

Third party motor vehicle insurance is compulsory in most countries. It is strongly recommended you contact your insurer to make sure you're adequately covered.

Most insurance policies issued in the UK automatically provide third party cover in EC countries as well as in some others. They do not provide comprehensive cover unless you arrange this with your insurer, who may charge an extra premium.

Make sure you have the appropriate insurance certificate with you.

Certain countries require a bail bond as a security in the event of an accident. Consult your insurer.

Your driving licence

You must carry your national driving licence when motoring abroad. Even if you need an International Driving Permit (see below), take your national licence also.

If you want to ride a hired or borrowed motorcycle in the country you're visiting, ask about minimum age requirements in case they apply to you.

Translation In Italy, you must carry either a translation with your licence or an International Driving Permit. If you have a pink or pink and green EC-type UK licence, this translation isn't required.

International Driving Permit (IDP)

Many non-EC countries still require an IDP.

To qualify for one, you must be 18 or over.

To apply you'll need

* your driving licence
* a passport-sized photograph
* a fee.

The motoring organisations can issue your IDP.

Vehicle Registration Document

You must carry the original Vehicle Registration Document with you.

If you don't have your Vehicle Registration Document, apply to a Vehicle Registration Office for a temporary certificate of registration (V379). Apply through your local Post Office well in advance of your journey.

If you plan to hire, borrow or lease a vehicle, you must ensure you have all the relevant documents.

Personal documents

Passport/visa

All persons travelling must either hold, or be named on, an up-to-date passport valid for all countries through which you intend to travel.

Carry your passport(s) at all times.

Keep a separate note of the number, date and place of issue of each passport, in case they are stolen or lost.

Travellers need a visa for some European countries. Check well in advance with the embassies or consulates concerned. This is particularly important if you hold a UK passport not issued in this country, or the passport of any other country.

Medical expenses insurance

You're strongly advised to take out comprehensive medical insurance cover for any trip abroad.

Most medical treatment can be obtained free of charge or at reduced cost from the healthcare schemes of countries with whom the UK has reciprocal healthcare arrangements.

However, don't rely on these arrangements alone.

Department of Health leaflet E111
Department of Health leaflet E111 is available from any Post Office. It provides health advice for travellers.

Motoring regulations

Drink and riding

Don't drink and ride. The laws and penalties abroad are often more severe than those in the UK.

Advance warning triangle

The use of a warning triangle is compulsory in most countries for all vehicles with more than two wheels (including side-car outfits). Hazard warning lights should not be used instead of a triangle, but to complement it. Some countries require two advance warning triangles.

Spare bulbs

Some countries require you to carry a spare set of bulbs.

First aid kit

Make sure your vehicle carries a first aid kit. It is compulsory in some countries and strongly recommended in many others.

Identification plate

If you're towing a trailer, fit an identification plate.

Nationality plate

You must display a nationality plate of the approved size and design at the rear of your motorcycle or trailer.

Speed limits

There are speed limits in all countries, but they vary from country to country.

A list of the speed limits can be obtained from the motoring organisations. Make sure you know the limits for those countries you will be travelling through.

Obey all speed limits. Many countries have severe on-the-spot fines for offenders. Others prosecute, and that could prove to be expensive.

Warning: police fines

On-the-spot fines are imposed for most minor motoring offences. Make sure you know the regulations for each country you intend visiting and obey them.

Riding in Europe

It can take you time to adjust to riding on the right. Mistakes can lead to accidents.

When taking rear observation remember you're now riding on the right. This is particularly important before deciding to overtake. Rear observation to the left is vitally important.

Make certain you feel fit enough for your trip. Don't let your attention wander. It can be dangerous to forget where you are, even for a moment.

Each time you set out, remember that you're in a foreign country where you must ride on the right.

Avoid riding for long periods and don't allow fatigue to set in.

Take special care after a rest when you return onto the road again.

Remember

Hire motorcycles may be unfamiliar.

Make sure you understand the controls layout before you ride.

After your trip

Don't forget to adjust to riding on the left again as soon as you return!

Defensive riding

- take extra care at roundabouts. Be aware of the changed priority
- don't attempt to overtake until you're used to riding on the right.

Motorway tolls

Some countries charge motorway tolls. Find out about these and include them in your budget.

Security

Loss of possessions, passports, tickets, cash and credit cards can be distressing and inconvenient when you're abroad.

Be on your guard against confidence tricksters.

Checklist

As part of your planning, make a checklist of equipment, documents and other items.

If you're travelling through several countries, check against each item whether it's compulsory or strongly recommended.

The topics covered

- a final word
- useful addresses.

SAFE RIDING FOR LIFE

A final word

Having studied this book, are **you** satisfied with your own standard of riding?

If you are satisfied, should you be?

Every one of us is capable of making mistakes on the road. However, not everyone is prepared to make allowances for those mistakes when they are committed by others.

Watch out for other people's mistakes and be ready to slow down or stop. Never rely on other road users doing the right thing. It's dangerous.

Always be critical of your own standard of riding before you comment on that of another. Ask yourself whether **you** always stick to the rules so that everyone else knows what to expect.

Remember, the perfect road user doesn't exist. Whatever stage you have reached as a motorcyclist, always aim for a higher standard.

Watch others and copy the best of what you see. Be tolerant of the worst, and learn how to avoid such errors yourself.

There is no place on today's roads for impatience, intolerance, exhibitionism, aggression or selfishness. If you behave in any of those ways, you create stress for yourself and could be well on your way to having an accident.

The ability to handle your vehicle and react quickly to road and traffic conditions doesn't necessarily make you either a good or a safe motorcyclist. Riding skill alone will not prevent accidents. Your attitude of mind is just as important, as is having a detailed knowledge of defensive riding techniques.

Developing the right attitude and behaviour is something you need to keep working at.

The good rider needs

- a sense of responsibility
- concentration on the job of riding correctly
- good anticipation
- patience and confidence.

Above all, show courtesy and consideration to **all** road users.

Reducing the risk of accidents will make our roads safer for everyone.
So make sure your aim is

'Safe riding for life'

DSA Test Enquiries and Booking Centre

DSA
PO Box 280
Newcastle-upon-Tyne NE99 1WE

Tel: 0870 01 01 372
Welsh speakers: 0870 01 00 372
Minicom users: 0870 01 07 372
Fax: 0870 01 02 372

www.driving-tests.co.uk

DSA Head Office

Stanley House
56 Talbot Street
Nottingham NG1 5GU

Tel: 0115 901 2500
Fax: 0115 901 2940

Driver and Vehicle Licensing Agency (DVLA)

www.dvla.gov.uk

Customer Enquiry Unit
Swansea SA6 7JL

Tel: 0870 240 0009
Fax: 01792 783071

Institute of Advanced Motorists

www.iam.org.uk

IAM House
359 Chiswick High Road
London W4 4H5

Tel: 020 8994 4403
Fax: 020 8994 9249

The Royal Society for the Prevention of Accidents (ROSPA)

www.rospa.co.uk

Edgbaston Park
353 Bristol Road
Birmingham B5 7ST

Tel: 0121 248 2000
Fax: 0121 248 2001

DSA MOTORCYCLE RIDING

DSA MOTORCYCLE RIDING

Passenger
   carrying 224–6, 228
      legal requirements 225
      motorcycle adjustments 225
      riding techniques 226
   clothing 226
   instructing 226
Patience 5, 165, 269
Pedestrian crossings 119–22, 178
   arm signals at 70
   pelican crossings 119, 121
   puffin crossings 119, 121
   rules and advice 120
   school crossing patrols 122, 178
   toucan crossings 119, 121
   zebra crossings 119, 121, 158
Pedestrians 97
   on bends 127, 129, 133
   children 178
   on country roads 174
   disabled 178, 179
   elderly 178
   at junctions 140, 168, 178
   at night 220
   at roundabouts 158
   at traffic lights 87
   visually handicapped people 178, 179
Penalty points 21
Pollution, effects of 252, 253, 254
Pollution, reducing 254–6
Position on the road (see Road position)
Position-Speed-Look (PSL) routine (see
   OSM/PSL routines)
Protection from cold 7, 32, 36, 38, 39, 210
Protection from wet weather 7, 32, 36, 39
Protective clothing (see Clothing, protective)
Provisional moped licence entitlement 14
Provisional motorcycle licence entitlement
   11

Reflective material 41, 176, 219
Reflective studs, coloured 83
Refresher training 8
Responsibility 4
Rider 2–9
   new 8
   returning 8
Riding, high-speed 116, 180
Riding ahead 96 (see also Anticipation;
   Observation, ahead)
Riding at night 216–23
   adjusting to darkness 217
   bends 135
   built up areas 220
   horn 220
   meeting other vehicles 223
   noise 220
   overtaking 221
   parking 222
   seeing 217
   wet roads 176
Riding conditions
   bad weather (see Weather)
   busy areas 98
   fog (see Fog)
   traffic 94–124
Riding position 61
Riding standard 8, 269
Road camber 130
Road humps 89
Road markings 82–6, 103
   in fog 209
   lines across the road 79, 80, 82, 86, 142
   lines along the road 82–3
   schools 85
   single broken lines 83
   speed reduction lines 86
   words on the road 85

Essential Reading

The Highway Code

The Highway Code is essential reading for everyone. It explains road traffic law and gives guidance as to best driving practice, with particular reference to vulnerable road users such as horse riders, cyclists and the elderly. The current version was prepared to reflect the changes in lifestyle and technology, giving rules for dealing with driver fatigue and recommendations about the use of mobile phones.

ISBN 0 11 552290 5   £1.49

Know Your Traffic Signs

This useful publication illustrates and explains the vast majority of traffic signals, signs and road markings which any road user is likely to encounter. It is the most comprehensive explanation of the signing system available, and is exceptional value for money.

ISBN 0 11 551612 3   £2.50

The Official Theory Test for Motorcyclists

A change to legislation from 1st February 2001 meant that anyone who wants to be eligible for a motorbike licence has to pass the motorcycle theory test before they do their practical motorcycle test. The change is part of the Government's road safety strategy to improve motorcycle safety.

The Official Theory Test for Motorcyclists contains the full question bank from which the questions for the motorbike theory test are taken.

ISBN 0 11 552227 1   £11.99

Official Motorcycling – CBT, Theory and Practical Test

This is a NEW product! It combines all the information the novice rider needs to know about compulsory basic training with all the instruction the motorcyclist needs in order to prepare for the practical test. It is the ONLY official product on the market dealing with both CBT and the practical test and an essential reference for anyone who wants to ride on the road.

ISBN 0 11 552258 1   £7.99

Order Form

5 easy ways to order:

- **Online:**   Visit www.**clicktso**.com
- **Tel:**   Please call **0870 600 5522** *quoting ref BAV*
- **Fax:**   Fax this form to **0870 600 5533**
- **Post:**   **TSO, PO Box 29,**
  Norwich NR3 1GN
- **TSO Bookshops:**   Visit your local TSO Bookshop

Please send me the following publications:

Title	ISBN	Price	Quantity
The Highway Code	0 11 552290 5	£1.49	....
Know Your Traffic Signs	0 11 551612 3	£2.50	....
The Official Theory Test for Motorcyclists	0 11 552227 1	£11.99	....
Official Motorcycling – CBT, Theory and Practical Test	0 11 552258 1	£7.99	....
Handling charge per order:		£3.00	
Total enclosed:		£..................	

PLEASE COMPLETE IN BLOCK CAPITALS

Name ....

Address ....

....

....

.... Postcode .... | BAV |

☐ I enclose a cheque for £.................... payable to: '*TSO*'

☐ Please charge to my account with TSO, No:

....

☐ Please debit my Mastercard/Visa/Amex/Diners/Connect Card Account No.

☐☐☐☐☐☐☐☐☐☐☐☐☐☐☐☐☐☐☐

Signature.. Expiry date ....

☐ Please send me information on TSO products. My email address is

....@..

Alternatively, contact us NOW to register at www.**clicktso**.com

☐ Please tick this box if you do not wish to receive
further information by conventional mail on
products and services from The Stationery Office.

Prices are correct at time of going to press but may be
subject to change without notice.
TSO account holders should note that credit card
transactions will not be shown on their statements.
A full listing of terms and conditions of sale can be
obtained on request from TSO, PO Box 29,
Norwich NR3 1GN.

TSO

DSA
DRIVING STANDARDS AGENCY
SAFE DRIVING FOR LIFE